The View from Lincoln Hill

The View

Man and the Land in a New England Town

with drawings by the author

from Lincoln Hill

BY PAUL BROOKS

HOUGHTON MIFFLIN COMPANY BOSTON 1976

BY PAUL BROOKS

Roadless Area

The Pursuit of Wilderness

The House of Life: Rachel Carson at Work

The View from Lincoln Hill: Man and the Land
in a New England Town

Book design by David Ford

The map appearing in Chapter 7 is by Samuel H. Bryant

Library of Congress Cataloging in Publication Data
Brooks, Paul.
    The view from Lincoln Hill.
    1. Lincoln, Mass.—History—Addresses, essays,
lectures. 2. Land—Massachusetts—Lincoln—Addresses,
essays, lectures. 3. Human ecology—Massachusetts
—Lincoln—Addresses, essays, lectures. I. Title.
F74.L7B77   974.4′4   76–12564
ISBN 0–395–24398–X

Printed in the United States of America

C 10 9 8 7 6 5 4 3 2 1

To the "Town Fathers," past and present, male and female, who have worked to make Lincoln what it is.

". . . Let us set out in the hope that our descendants
may say it has been not less well with them than it was
with us and with our fathers. It is a goodly land; and
may they in their day feel blest in its possession, no less
than do we in ours."

— Charles Francis Adams   Anniversary Address,
  Lincoln, 1904

AUTHOR'S NOTE

Parts of this book have appeared in *The New York Times*, in *Man and Nature* (the annual publication of the Massachusetts Audubon Society), in *Country Journal*, in Herbert W. Gleason's *Thoreau Country*, in *Audubon*, in *Smithsonian*, and in *The Living Wilderness*. The section entitled "Trial by Fire" was privately published for Lincoln citizens by the Lincoln 1975 Bicentennial Commission, as part of the town's observance of the anniversary.

Facts and names of largely local interest have been placed in the notes at the back, together with a list of the principal sources for each chapter. I acknowledge with many thanks the contributions of friends in Lincoln (which are included in this section of the book) and the constructive comments by the best of editors, my wife. The notes on the last chapter, "Room for Living," give further information about Lincoln's current land conservation program.

Contents

The Birth of a Community

CHAPTER 1 ⌐

"There is a good view of Lincoln lying high up in among the hills.
You see that it is the highest town hereabouts, and hence its fruit."
— Henry David Thoreau

"If we abandon our New England heritage, we do so at our peril."
— Sumner Chilton Powell, *Puritan Village*

A Sense of Place

"A place is more than so many cubic feet of earth." The place referred to was Lincoln, Massachusetts, fifteen miles west of Boston; the occasion was the dedication, on a May morning in 1892, of the new town hall. Twelve years later, at the sesquicentennial celebration of the town's founding, the speaker was more explicit. "The dwellers in the homes of their fathers . . . inherit something which is not known among the changing population of a city or its suburbs." Today only a small minority of Lincoln's five thousand inhabitants live in the homes of their fathers, and by most definitions the town would have to be called a suburb.

Yet Lincoln has, in recent years, been widely cited as an example of a community that has somehow managed to maintain rural values in the face of mounting urban pressure; that has controlled its rate of growth, preserved its open space, and successfully resisted the type of ruthless exploitation that sees land merely as a commodity in the market. How has this come about?

If the substance of Lincoln's story were purely local — a wine that could not travel — there would be little point in writing about it. But it appears that Lincoln's experience is closely related to that of thousands of towns throughout the United States: towns with roots in the past, determined to maintain their character and identity while at the same time making their contribution to the larger community of which they are a part. Lincoln is not unique in seeking to shape its future rather than passively allowing the future to shape it. Granted, the tools at our command differ somewhat from those in other parts of the country. Local chisels are sharp in New England, and the time-honored town meeting wields a formidable mallet which may elsewhere be in the less sensitive hand of the county or the state. But the individual citizen, in concert with his neighbors, is everywhere the sculptor, regardless of the legal structure within which he works. Basic principles of land use and town planning are universal, and creative ideas for implementing them gain rather than lose weight through circulation. No single town can lay claim to any magic formula, or special expertise. Yet with its long history of public service and its present state of awareness, Lincoln has proved a fertile seedbed for such ideas.

Lincoln is first of all a New England town; only recently, by accident of geography and economics, a suburb of Boston. Like its famous neighbor, Concord, it grew up as a farming community with, however, many of the intellectual concerns we tend nowadays to associate with city life. Made up from parts of three adjacent townships (hence the forgotten sobriquet, "Niptown"), it was finally incorporated in 1754, two decades after the local inhabitants had sent their petition to the General Court, "setting forth their difficulties and inconveniences by reason of their distance from the places of Public Worship in their respective Towns." This rural origin has direct bearing on the appearance of Lincoln today. Because the new village was established in an outlying district, there is no heavily built-up town center; broad fields surround the central five corners, and run up the very slopes of Lincoln Hill. Though the farms are disappearing, we still have open meadows and pasture land, undrained swamps and bogs, unpolluted

ponds, and a few bits of mature forest. Despite a doubling
of population in the last twenty years, Lincoln remains one
of the last green islands in an encroaching sea of urban
sprawl.

This has not happened by chance. It is partly a matter of
continuity. One family, for example, still holds title to its
land through a proprietor's grant from the Massachusetts
Bay Colony. From earliest times, the principal landowners
took for granted their responsibility to the town, as witness the family whose members served in the same office —
father, son, grandson, great-grandson — for a century and a
half. Thus grew up the tradition that still leads so many
Lincoln residents, at one time or another, to participate in
local government. Towns like Lincoln represent something
that is steadily disappearing from American life — a sense
of place. Americans are the most mobile people on earth:
every year approximately one family in five changes its
residence. Like trees grown in a nursery, our roots are
kept trimmed close to the trunk against the day when we
shall be transplanted. The implications of this fact for the
individual and for society are familiar enough. Less obvious, perhaps, is its bearing on the basic truth that has re-
emerged in this "age of ecology": the interdependence of
man and his environment. The frontier philosophy of "exploit and move on" became obsolete with the disappearance
of the frontier itself. But the concept of land as a commodity — as "so many cubic feet of earth" — is far from
dead. It is gruesomely apparent on a national scale in the
over-cutting of our forests, the strip-mining of our mountains, the drowning of our river valleys, the poisoning of
the land and the water and the air above it. Less spectacular is the steady erosion of local communities whose roots
are not deep enough to withstand the pressures of outside
exploitation. Those near great cities are clearly most
threatened. They will not be saved by statute. And if they

are lost, the city itself will be the loser. As one student of urban affairs wrote recently: "It may well be that the only answer to the nation's urban problems is to find ways to restore a sense of community in metropolitan neighborhoods where it has vanished or been destroyed." Better still to cherish it where it still exists.

This "sense of community" made the early settlements possible, and the ways in which it was preserved have an obvious lesson for today. If terms like "urban sprawl" and "green belt" were unknown to the colonists, they were nonetheless well aware of the concepts involved. "The Puritans," writes Lewis Mumford, "knew and applied a principle that Plato had long ago pointed out in *The Republic*, namely, that an intelligent and socialized community will continue to grow only as long as it can remain a unit and keep up its common institutions. . . When the corporation has a sufficient number of members, that is to say, when the land is fairly occupied, and when the addition of more land would unduly increase the hardship of working it from the town, or would spread out the farmers and make it difficult for them to attend to their religious and civic duties, the original settlement throws out a new shoot. So Charlestown threw off Woburn; so Dedham colonized Medfield; so Lynn founded Nahant. . ." And so, as the Bay Colony grew, many new towns were born, each with its own church and civil government and its sense of identity.

Though the past is very much alive in Lincoln, I have not attempted to compile a town history. Rather I have sought to create a portrait which may have some documentary value, perhaps even some immediate usefulness, when looked at from the outside. The material itself is specific, local, concrete. Though statistical studies in suburban development, land use, population curves, and traffic patterns are doubtless as fascinating to the professional

planner as computerized head measurements of Hottentots
are to the anthropologist, most of us would rather get to
know one Hottentot well and extrapolate from him. Fortunately Lincoln, as part of the greater Concord region, is
closely associated with key events and characters in American history, both political and cultural. Here the American revolution began. Here, some two generations later,
American literature made its declaration of independence.
Cultural movements do not recognize town lines, and it
seems appropriate to include a chapter on the Concord writers and their relation to the land as a part of the Lincoln
tradition.

Every town has its own personality. A century and a
quarter ago, Thoreau — who could be quite caustic about
men who lived "lives of quiet desperation" — remarked
that "the inhabitants of Lincoln yield sooner than usual to
the influence of the rising generation, and are a mixture of
rather simple but clever with a well-informed and trust-
worthy people." The mix, let us hope, has not greatly
changed.

CHAPTER 2 ⌉

"The study of landscapes is a good beginning for the study of the societies of men, because men must live on and off the land as the first condition of their survival."
— George Caspar Homans, *English Villagers of the Thirteenth Century*

"When we walk, we naturally go to the fields and woods; what would become of us, if we walked only in a garden or a mall?"
— Henry David Thoreau

The Living Landscape

Like other young couples before and since, my wife and I first came to know Lincoln as a place to walk. Cooped up in a Cambridge apartment during the week, we would often head west on Sundays toward the nearest stretch of open country. Here were narrow roads bordered by oaks or elms or neat rows of old sugar maples, the roadway separated from broad hayfields or pasture or plowland by stone walls that showed the hand of the craftsman. Here were paths through the pine woods, small streams and swamps and bogs, and two sizable ponds (elsewhere they would be called lakes) in addition to famous Walden Pond on the Concord line. Here was a hill clad in paper birch and hemlock such as one might come upon in the wilds of New Hampshire, from the top of which one could look down on the Sudbury River. Here even at the built-up center, just below the hill, lay the open expanse of the town park.

The spaciousness we found so near the city we doubtless took for granted. For this was over forty years ago, before Lincoln was truly a suburb. When shortly we came to live here, we automatically spoke of "living in the country," to the amusement of our city friends. Farms still flourished, large estates remained unbroken, and the need for a formal program to save open land must have seemed remote to all but the most foresighted of the town fathers.

This sense of spaciousness is enhanced by the fact that Lincoln village, in typical New England style, is set upon a hill. Settled before the exodus from the city, the hilltop itself has suffered little during the present century from the violent winds of change. Today I find it as good a spot as any from which to seek a perspective on the broader landscape of which it is a part: a landscape that shaped the lives of our forebears and that still can, if we give it a fair chance, shape our own.

A friend of mine from the West, seeing New England for the first time, remarked that this is a gentle land. To be sure, it was spring; of the long, hard winter just past, the only trace was a patch or two of sodden snow in the darkest part of the wood, here and there a sapling still bent to the ground or the raw wound of a branch torn off by the wind. Visiting Englishmen have had a different reaction; to them our climate and our landscape are both a bit out of control. Yet compared to much of America, the New England countryside is indeed undramatic, understated. One need only contrast Henry Thoreau's painstaking search for wildness and truth in the fields and swamps of Concord with John Muir's glory in the sharp peaks and sudden storms of the High Sierra.

By western standards our mountains are low and soft in outline; once massive ranges, they were already worn down and mellowed by age when the Rockies and the Sierras were born. The rolling hills of southern New England tend to reach a uniform height in any one area, suggesting to geologists that they are the remnants of what was originally a high, level plain. Only the occasional monadnock of harder rock, once the highest peak along a watershed, rises like a solitary island in a sea of green. Indeed, the view from the top of Lincoln Hill gives a deceptive appearance of flatness as distant hilltops blend in the bluish haze, broken to the westward by the rounded mass of Mount Wachusett and, on a clear day, by the prototype of such formations, Mount Monadnock itself.

The hill on which we are standing has a northeast-southwest orientation, as have most of the hills in Lincoln and elsewhere in Massachusetts, apparently related to the wrinkling of the bedrock that accompanied the formation of the Appalachian mountain system. It was given its present contour and surface composition quite recently, as geologic time is measured, by the action of the glacier that once covered all of New England, and which bequeathed to our region its heritage of natural ponds and bogs and "glacial kettles" (including famous Walden Pond), of ancient lake beds (our principal stone-free areas), of eskers, drumlins, and moraines. Moving across the land from north-northwest to south-southeast, the ice smoothed the hills at the point of contact but tore off huge blocks from the leeward side. Hence the steep slope dropping down from the hilltop reservoir to the fertile flatland of Flint's farm lying below us to the southeast — land granted in colonial days to the great-great-great-great-great-great grandfather of the present owner. The town stands at the watershed of three rivers, the Concord, the Charles, and the Shawsheen; as an early historian put it, "not a tubful of water comes into the town from any source except the rains and dews of heaven." Though Henry Thoreau, looking across country from a vantage point in the Sudbury River valley, noted in his journal that Lincoln is "the highest town hereabouts," its summit is only 390 feet above sea level. Perhaps he considered this sufficient to make its "fruit" superior to that of a larger town where men are "so occupied with the factitious cares and superfluously coarse labors of life that its finer fruits cannot be plucked by them." No doubt he liked the comparative remoteness of the village, and its rocky sparseness in contrast to Concord's lush meadows and busy main street, thinking it a good place to learn how much you can get along without.*

Thoreau had grown up at a time when the thin soils of New England were being used to capacity; during the early years of the nineteenth century there was more cleared land than ever before or since. Plowland, meadows for grazing cattle, and sheep pasture were all under intensive use. Farm products found a ready market in towns growing up around local industries, and with agricultural prosperity came a flowering of domestic architecture and — in Concord especially — of the literary arts. A passage from Emerson's *Nature*, written some years earlier, suggests — while noting the great number of farms — that the value of the rural landscape was not wholly economic: "The charming landscape I saw this morning is indubitably made up of some twenty or thirty farms. Miller owns this field, Locke that, and Manning the woodland beyond. But none of them owns the landscape. There is a property in the horizon which no man has but he whose eye can integrate all the parts, that is, the poet. This is the best of these men's farms, yet to this their warranty-deeds give no title."

It was fine while it lasted. But the best part of the farms had no market value, and in the long run the sparse soil that covers so much of New England has done better in growing character than in growing crops. Granted, there was much variety, as an early settler remarked: "The soyle I judge to be lusty and fat in many places, light and hot, in some places sandy botomed and some loomy." But the up-

---

* The following description of Lincoln in the early nineteenth century is perhaps overly stark. "The old road [Trapelo] leading to the town of Lincoln, for the last six miles, is crooked, narrow, and hilly, little travelled and much neglected. The roads within the limits of the town are generally uneven and in bad repair. The soil is coarse and rocky, a great portion whereof is covered with wood, and not more than one third of the town under culture."
— John G. Hales, *A Survey of Boston and Its Vicinity*

land sandy loam soils were essentially infertile. The fields were full of rocks, the clearings comparatively small and unsuited to large-scale mechanized agriculture. Farms in New England could be profitable only so long as they had no serious competition. Quite suddenly, in midcentury, the competition materialized.

Two momentous events had occurred: the building of the Erie Canal, and the opening of the railroad from Boston to Albany. It is a curious fact of history that one of the greatest influences in shaping our landscape and our economy should have been an engineering triumph beyond our borders. Completed in 1825, the canal soon began supplying New England markets with produce from the deep, rich soils of the Midwest. Within a few decades, New England farmers were beginning to feel the pinch. By 1840, western wheat was being used by the farmers themselves as well as by city people. In one well-studied area of Massachusetts, at least half the land under cultivation in 1850 was abandoned during the next twenty years. Pastures so laboriously cleared for the raising of sheep grew up once more to forest: in many areas to almost pure stands of white pine, whose light windborne seeds found a perfect seedbed in the sun-drenched sod (where hardwoods could not take hold) and which, when they came of age, were in their turn felled to feed the sawmills throughout southern New England in the early years of this century.

And so the complex sequence goes on, and the pattern of the landscape slowly changes over the years. Cut-over pine woods are succeeded by the shade-tolerant seedlings of deciduous trees like oak and maple and birch — which grow up to provide the subtle colors of spring and the spectacular fall display that uprooted Yankees inevitably recall with nostalgia. Yet the noble white pine persists. As I have learned in my own woodlot, a single seed tree is enough to repopulate the entire neighborhood if one thins the hard-

woods — in this case, the locally dominant red oak — sufficiently to let in the light. Old, gnarled pines, some broader
than they are high, flourish along the stone walls at the
pasture's edge; others have taken root in midfield, cheek by
jowl with the ubiquitous red cedar. In her charming little
book, *The Changing Face of New England*, the botanist
Betty Flanders Thomson points out that the northern
boundary of the oak forest "apparently lies a little to the
north of the boundary between old-field red cedar and old-
field white pine. . . A forestry professor amused himself
during a year of commuting between Boston and New
Haven by driving a different route on each trip and mark-
ing the pine-cedar boundary on a map." Since both trees
take root in our abandoned fields (though the red cedar
generally comes first), I imagine that his line of demarca-
tion must have run more or less through Lincoln. In any
case, the process of natural reforestation — often by scrubby
and worthless "weed trees" — has been continuing in our
part of the world for more than a century. And now in
Lincoln, as the last of our farms disappear, the maintenance
of open grasslands and broad vistas is becoming a major
concern.

This game of reconstructing vanished landscapes has
more than academic interest as we study problems of "land
use" in towns like Lincoln which within a generation or
two have changed from rural to suburban communities, yet
whose rural character their residents are determined to
save. The game has involved botanists and others in some
fascinating detective work which, in dispelling certain mis-
conceptions of our countryside's past, may help us to anticipate its future. For example, the widespread belief that the
early settlers on our shores found themselves in a primeval
forest consisting wholly of huge and ancient trees has
proved to be a myth. Studies at the Harvard Forest in
Petersham indicate that there have been at least four major

hurricane blow-downs in New England within the last five hundred years, all of them as severe as the 1938 hurricane that flattened so much of our forest, especially the shallow-rooted and unbending white pine. One such storm occurred toward the end of the fifteenth century — which means that most of the woodland that greeted our Puritan forebears was only about a hundred and fifty years old. Of Petersham itself, some forty-five miles to the west of us, the former Director of the Harvard Forest, Hugh Raup, writes: "When the first settlers came to Petersham in 1733, most of the forests they found here had to be between 80 and 130 years old, and descriptions written in the 1700's show that the species composition and the species distribution in the land-scape were essentially the same as at present." Of course there must have been many ancient groves, as well as huge individual trees like the white pines that were blazed with the King's Broad Arrow to reserve them for masts for the Royal Navy.* (A growing source of resentment toward Britain in northern New England.) There were also clear-ings in the forest made by the Indians, who from time to time deliberately set fires to burn out the undergrowth and blow-downs. And there were the rich grassy bottomlands, which greatly influenced the choice of location for the early settlements inland, the first of which was our mother town, Concord.

Though New England has changed greatly over the cen-turies, it is perhaps easier for us standing on Lincoln Hill to visualize earlier landscapes than it would be in some other parts of America. The West still has a few great tracts of pure wilderness, as we alas do not, but where the land has been exploited, it is permanently changed beyond recognition. Wheat fields stretch to the horizon where once

* It is sad to realize that in 1925, when the frigate *Constitution* was re-fitted, there were no white pines left in the East tall enough to replace her original masts felled in the forests of Maine. Three great Douglas firs had to be brought all the way from the Northwest.

there was prairie; forests have been clear-cut; valleys have been drowned. Here in Massachusetts, man's war on nature has been less violent, and there has been more chance for regeneration. The threat to the future of our landscape is of a different kind: the population explosion, and urban sprawl. In seeking to see today's problem in perspective, one must sooner or later deal with the fundamental question of man's attitude toward the land, as it was shaped by European civilization, philosophy, and religion. One aspect of this broad and complex subject comes very close to home: the attitude of the first settlers toward the wilderness, and its effect, in turn, on them. How it looked to them may not be too hard to imagine. How they felt about it — which bears on how we still think about the natural environment — is a more complicated matter.

In the history of Western culture, in contrast to that of the East, untamed nature has been looked upon with varying degrees of distaste, ranging from indifference to actual hostility and fear. "Wilderness," in the Old Testament sense, was equated with "desert": a haunt of evil spirits, a place of trial. Ordered gardens, parks, pastoral landscapes were beautiful; wild scenery was ugly, and menacing. Not until some two hundred years ago — about the time of the American Revolution — did this attitude begin to change, as European philosophers and poets learned to appreciate the beauty in wildness and to recognize man's kinship with the rest of nature. When New England was being settled, the Biblical injunction to subdue the earth, which doubtless dates back to early man's evolution from a hunting to a farming culture, was still taken literally. Witness the ruling of the Massachusetts General Court in 1652 defining the Indians' right of possession: "What lands any of the Indians within this jurisdiction have by possession or improvement, by subduing of the same, they have just right thereto, according to that in Genesis, 1 and 28, Chapter 9:1, and Psalms 115:16." Incredibly, this concept persists today at the very core of our environmental troubles.

This is not to say that the Puritans necessarily came here with the intention of chopping down trees and subduing the wilderness. Apparently they had little idea of what they were getting in for. Promotional literature made America sound like a potential Garden of Eden. John Smith touted the virtues of the new land where any man of "sense, strength and health" could provide for his sustenance with "a little extraordinary labor." John White in *The Planter's Plea* extolled the natural abundance of the forest, the fertility of the soil and even the salubriousness of the climate: "No Countrey yeelds a more propitious ayre for our temper, than New-England . . ." The Reverend Francis Higginson, describing "our new Paradise of New England" (which he visited only in the summer) could scarcely restrain himself: "Experience doth manifest that there is hardly a more healthfull place to be found in the World . . . This Countrey aboundeth naturally with store of Rootes of great varietie and good to eat. Our Turnips, Parsnips and Carrots are here both bigger and sweeter then is ordinarily to bee found in *England*. Here are stores of Pumpions, Cowcombers, and other things of that nature which I know not . . . The fertilitie of the Soyle is to be admired at, as appeareth in the aboundance of Grasse that groweth everie where both verie thicke, verie long, and verie high in divers places . . . the aboundant encrease of Corne proves this Countrey to bee a wonderment . . . Both Land and Sea abound with store of blessings for the comfortable sustenance of Mans life in *New England*."

Experience, alas, manifested otherwise. "The good Land," as John Winthrop called it, turned out to be "wilde and overgrown with woods." As the settlers fought for survival, preconceived ideas gave way to reality. One disillusioned colonist wrote: "The air of the country is sharp, the rocks many, the trees innumerable, the wolves at midnight howling." The Puritans' dedication to the building of a new Zion in America was soon put to the test. If New England were to become a garden, it would have to be by man's own heroic efforts. Here religious faith strengthened the heart and gave a deeper bite to the ax. The wilderness was a place of temptation, the Devil's domain. To subdue it was not only a practical necessity, it was holy work.

Why then, as the facts became known, did settlers continue to come to New England? "There was no reason except religion to make Englishmen prefer New England to Barbados or Virginia," writes Samuel Eliot Morison in *Builders of the Bay Colony.* "Free land was more easily obtained in the Southern colonies than in New England, and far more productive when you got it." The founders of the Bay Colony themselves sought to counteract the real estate propaganda that encouraged "the poorer sort" to settle here in hope of profit. "If any come hither to plant for worldly ends, that can live well at home, he commits an error, of which he will soon repent him," wrote Thomas Dudley, the first Deputy Governor, to the Countess of Lincoln, "but if for spiritual . . . he may find here what may well content him."* John White had already stressed the holy nature of the struggle: "Colonies have their warrant from God's direction and command . . . to replenish the earth, and to subdue it."

God's will conveniently coincided with the other basic motive for colonization: individual land ownership. To a middle class immigrant from England, where great land holdings were the source of wealth, power and prestige, the possession of one's own acres, to do with as one saw fit, must have represented the ultimate satisfaction this side of

* Dudley's letter is dated March 12, 1630. He apologizes that, in writing, he "must do so rudely, having yet no table, nor other room to write in, than by the fire-side upon my knee, in this sharp winter."

heaven. Accepted as a basic human right, land ownership is obviously closely linked with the development of democracy and individual liberties; the landowner knew that he was as good as his neighbor, and perhaps a mite better. In New England it hastened the secularization of the theocratic government. And certainly the desire to own land — which in the Puritan colonies could be held in fee simple, without quitrent — was one of the principal drives behind the mass migration that took place, largely from the economically depressed areas of England, during the decades immediately following the founding of the Massachusetts Bay Colony.

Limitless land, free for the taking, was a prime ingredient of what was later called the "American dream." The pioneer with his ax was to become the symbol of sturdy independence. Throughout North America, sins innumerable are still being committed in the name of a "free enterprise" society, where the title deed to one's land is the next thing to holy writ. "Land is one of the Gods of New England," wrote Roger Williams. But here in New England we at least have an example to guide us, if we will heed it. The pious Puritan, grubbing for his living in the spare soil, may seem a drab figure alongside Daniel Boone or Davy Crockett. But he had brought with him a sense of community, a disciplined social structure which was, from the very beginning, to govern his use of the limited resources at his command. He also brought a deeply ingrained tradition of husbandry from his English forebears. His settlements were planned from the outset with specific reference to the best uses of the available terrain. Not by chance was the colonial New England town, in the words of a leading social historian, "the only successfully blended beauty of natural and man-made environment that America has ever known."

CHAPTER 3 ⏋

"A race of hunters can never withstand the inroads of a race of husbandmen. The latter burrow in the night into their country and undermine them . . ."
— Henry David Thoreau

The First "Owners"

I referred to the land "free for the taking," but how free was it? No one can discuss land use anywhere in America, whether in Lincoln, Massachusetts, or in Lincoln, Nebraska, without eventually working back to the original "owners," the American Indians. And when one does so, one is immediately involved in complex moral and philosophical questions about which historians are not wholly in agreement even to this day.

One point is clear: the Indian and the European had wholly different concepts of man's relation to the earth. Neither the most friendly negotiations (such as took place at the beginning), nor the most solemn treaties, could ever make them understand each other. The Indian saw himself as inseparable from the natural world, as part of a divine order which he had no compulsion to "improve." I daresay that phrases like "man and nature" would have been quite incomprehensible to him. His association with the land, his identification with other living creatures, was in the deepest sense religious. Conservationists today like to speak of our "rape" of the land; from the Indian's point of view the earlier term "desecration" would be more accurate, for the land was sacred. Like the Eskimo, the Indian killed only for need; in ritual phrases he apologized to the animal whose life he sacrificed for his own survival. These rituals of thanksgiving applied also to the world of trees and plants, and the sense of oneness extended even to inanimate objects. In the words of a present-day Sioux: "The land-use philosophy of Indians is so utterly simple that it seems stupid to repeat it: man must live with other forms of life and not destroy it . . ."

Of course it is easy to wax sentimental about the "noble savage," as Jean Jacques Rousseau did from a distance of three thousand miles, and as modern writers do from a distance of three centuries in time. To claim that civilized society, which depends on large-scale agriculture, could exist without disturbing the natural scene would be absurd. But the fact remains that the truths known instinctively to the American Indians and other aboriginal peoples are the same that we are seeking to recapture today — both by means of sophisticated scientific studies, and through a mystical approach to the universe on the part of a growing body of thinkers (including some scientists) who are not afraid to use the word "love."

The first and fundamental clash between the culture of the early settlers and that of the existing inhabitants involved the concept of legal possession of territory. If the contradiction was not immediately apparent, this was because neither group knew what the other was talking about. How could a people who saw their ancestral land as sacrosanct, as an aspect of the supernatural, at the same time consider it subject to sale and to individual ownership? How could they be expected to see land as a commodity: a concept which is quite recent even in European history? When they "sold" their land, did they know what they were selling?

Recent apologists for the Puritan position claim that the Algonquian Indians, who practiced husbandry and had more or less permanent settlements, did indeed recognize a modified form of land ownership on the part of the tribe or

the family, if not of the individual. Tribes and villages un-
questionably possessed territorial rights, but they apparently were rights of *use*, not complete title in the European
sense. (There is also evidence that these territories were to
some extent adaptations to conditions imposed by the European fur trade.) In any case, such territories did not
represent land to be made over or exploited as the temporary "owners" saw fit; they were managed rather as trusts,
by a people with an intimate knowledge of the natural resources to be conserved and passed on to future members
of the tribe.

The wisdom of this attitude is easy to recognize with
hindsight — though it has taken us some three centuries to
do so. It was not so evident to the first settlers. As one tries

to reconstruct the colonial experience, the inevitable picture which emerges is that of land-hungry European multi-
tudes, sure of their secular and divine right to property, set
down in the midst of a savage Stone Age culture. By settling and "civilizing" this heathen land, these Englishmen
were doing God's work. And they felt quite secure in their
rights.

There was, of course, the right of discovery. Under a
Christian sovereign, unless the natives were already Christians, they didn't count. Furthermore, they had no valid
claim on land that they had not "subdued." As John Winthrop put it, "they ramble over much land without title or
property." (This concept of the nomadic Indian was used
until quite recent times to justify usurping Indian territory.
But it clearly did not apply to the settled villages and cultivated land of the eastern seaboard.) The Biblical concept
of wilderness as evil automatically made its inhabitants the
children of Satan. And if the initial friendliness of the
"children of Satan" toward the true Christians seemed like
a paradox, this was easily explained. It was God's doing.
"Though I cannot say that God sent a raven to feed us, as he
did the prophet Elijah," wrote Captain Roger Clap, "yet he
sent . . . Indians, which came with their baskets of corn on
their backs to trade with us — God caused the Indians to
help us with fish at very cheap rates."

To take over their land, which in any case they were not
"improving," was to serve God and spread the Gospel.
Though John White saw Indians as "men transferred into
beasts," they were still men, and it was the Puritan's duty
to convert them to Christianity. In his farewell sermon to
the company aboard the *Arbella*, John Cotton, vicar of St.
Botolph's Church in Boston, had exhorted them to "offend
not the poor Natives, but as you partake in their land, so
make them partakers of your precious faith."

Convinced of their legal and moral right to an untamed

wilderness, the Puritans were nevertheless at great pains to purchase the land for each new town. Though the record shows that our ancestors did not "steal" the land from the Indians, or cozen them into selling it for worthless trinkets, it would be unrealistic to claim that the American natives understood the meaning of property in European law. To be sure, the land they sold with solemn ceremony in exchange for the white man's products seldom included their cultivated fields; it was hunting and fishing ground, and these occupations they might continue to pursue within limits. Individual dealings between colonists and Indians were discouraged; after 1634 all land purchases had to be approved by the General Court.

The Indians on their part did not at first look upon the English as invaders or usurpers. (The Narragansetts had a simple explanation for their coming: obviously they had run out of firewood at home.) Indeed there was a tendency to welcome them as potential allies against neighboring hostile tribes. The Indians, wrote Francis Higginson in 1630, "doe generally professe to like well of our comming and planting here; partly because there is abundance of ground that they cannot posesse nor make use of, and partly because our being heere will bee a meanes both of reliefe to them when they want, and also a defence from their Enemies, wherewith (I say) before this Plantation began, they were often indangered." What a people who had lived so long in harmony with the life around them could not be expected to understand, nor could the English themselves be expected to consider, was the speed with which the Indian hunting grounds would shrink, and the fish and game disappear, under sheer pressure of numbers from abroad.

The Puritans had no immediate problem of dispossession. The Lord had made room for His people by visiting the heathen with a terrible plague just before the colonists arrived. In 1612 or thereabouts an epidemic of enormous proportions and of unknown character or origin (though probably inadvertently introduced by the English) destroyed a large proportion of the Indian population of southern New England, leaving the remainder weak and disorganized. The land was conveniently there for the taking; no need to fight for it, since "divine providence made way for the quiet and peaceable settlement of the English in those nations." And only a year or two before the beginning of settlement in Concord a smallpox epidemic killed off thousands of Indians and in some cases exterminated whole villages. "For the natives," wrote Governor Winthrop to a friend in England, "they are all dead of the small Poxe, so as the Lord hathe cleared our title to what we possess." The fact that only two white families suffered demonstrated, as the Governor put it, that God was "pleased with our inheriting these parts" for otherwise "why dothe he still make roome for us, by diminishing them as we increase?"

From the earliest days of the Bay Colony, Governor Winthrop had treated the Indian chieftains with dignity, provided they knew their place. "His solemnity of manner," writes Edward S. Morgan in *The Puritan Dilemma*, "was precisely the attitude to win their respect, and he took care that relations be on his terms, not theirs . . . He noted of one sachem, who visited him with a gift of corn, that 'being in English clothes, the Governor set him at his own table, where he behaved himself as soberly, etc., as an Englishman.' "

The white Americans' subsequent treatment of the Indian has ranged from ruthless suppression — such as the extermination of the Pequots in 1637 and later the calculated slaughter of the buffalo to starve the Plains tribes into submission — to patient and conscientious attempts at fair dealing. Though later generations may have considered that the only good Indian was a dead Indian, this was cer-

tainly not the attitude of the first settlers on the Atlantic
seaboard. Records of the Plymouth Colony indicate that
the Pilgrims dealt justly with the natives according to their
lights. Though the English considered the Indians an inferior race, they were no more strict with them than they
were with each other. This achievement of coexistence
— on which the newcomers' very survival depended —
smoothed the way for the Puritans in Massachusetts ten
years later. In a recent study of Puritan–Indian relations
before King Philip's War, Alden T. Vaughan concludes
that "the New England Puritans followed a remarkably
humane, considerate, and just policy in their dealings with
the Indians." Instructions from the Massachusetts Bay
Company specified that no injury "in the least kinde" be
done to the heathen. By contrast, a century and a half later,
George Washington had a different reason for keeping on
good terms with the Indians. To attempt to drive them
from their lands "is like driving the Wild Beasts of the Forest which will return . . . the gradual extension of our Settlements will as certainly cause the Savage as the Wolf to
retire; both being beasts of prey tho' they differ in shape."

The long, tragic history of our disposession of the American Indian tends to make us forget that there was a period
of comparatively peaceful coexistence before the two cul-

tures, so disparate in their view of the world, came inevitably into conflict. Plymouth and Boston achieved their initial foothold in the wilderness thanks to the Indian's good will. Devoted missionaries like John Eliot, author of the Indian Bible, converted many to Christianity; these "Praying Indians" became on occasion valuable allies. Concord, the first inland settlement, was to enjoy forty years of grace before the frontier suddenly burst into flame. The turning point — in retrospect the point of no return — was King Philip's War, which broke out in 1675. By that time the Indians were beginning to feel pushed around. Slowly they were being crowded out, resettled at the white man's pleasure. The settlers' cows were eating their corn. Their principal source of trade with the whites, furs, were becoming scarce, and they were temperamentally unable to become farmers, or to accept the Puritan work ethic. As friction intensified, all that was needed was a bold leader to spark a cruel and bloody war — if such a term can be applied to the harassment of the outlying settlements of a colony of some 120,000 inhabitants by warriors from nearby tribes totaling perhaps 1800 in all. The Indians found such a leader in Philip, chief of the Wampanoags, son of Massasoit, who had befriended the Pilgrims in the first hard years of the Plymouth Plantation. The "war" was short-lived, but the atrocities committed by both sides were such as to make a trusting relationship forever after impossible. Indians were not only savages; in European eyes, they were no longer human. While repelling ambushes in the forest, complained Increase Mather, the colonists often had to fire blindly, "whereby it is verily feared they did sometimes unhappily shoot Men instead of Indians."

Once the native Americans had been officially recognized as wild beasts, the next step was to offer bounties for their extermination. At the rate of a hundred pounds per scalp, this glorified form of market gunning could be very profitable, albeit risky. During the French and Indian Wars the Massachusetts legislature, with characteristic thoroughness, established a detailed scale of payments, beginning with children over the age of twelve.

But all this still lay in the future. When a brave band of Englishmen, only five years after the incorporation of the Bay Colony, resolved to try their fortunes amid the wilderness inland from the coast, they were justified in believing that their frontier settlement could live up to the name of Concord.

CHAPTER 4 ⌐

"Away Up in the Woods"

Concord, Lincoln's principal mother town, lies less than four miles northwest of Lincoln Hill as the crow flies (if crows flew in a straight line, which they seldom do). On flat land bordering the river, it is cut off from our sight by intervening hills. Founded in 1635, Concord was the first inland settlement in New England, and it is a prime example of the importance of local geography in determining the siting and the pattern of growth of a new community. Moreover, the very fact of its founding says a good deal about the Puritan's awareness, from the start, of the need for what we should call "planned development."

Why should the English, so soon after settling in the Massachusetts Bay area, seek new territory "away up in the woods" (in the words of a contemporary), far from the coastal fisheries, divorced from the neighborliness and protection of nearby towns, in an unknown country wholly surrounded by Indian lands? For one thing, there was already a land shortage, at least in the eyes of the original owners. In 1635, a few months before the settlement of Concord, the freemen of Watertown, declaring that their town had too many inhabitants "and the Town thereby in danger to be *ruinated*," passed a vote to protect themselves from a further influx of "forrainers." Newcomers — and nearly all Concord's founders emigrated directly from England — had better find their own land, beyond the boundaries of the existing plantations.

In retrospect, we can see that this strict local control over population growth helped to maintain closely knit communities, each with its own identity: something that has disappeared from so much of America. At the same time it preserved open land between town centers. Instead of sprawling over the countryside as population increased, the early New England town sent out shoots from the original rootstock, each of which developed into a new town: a pattern of land use incorporating the "green belt" concept that has become national policy in England today.

Fortunately for the newcomers, the country inland from the sea was not solid sunless forest; at least one open river basin was known to exist nearby. William Wood, whose *New Englands Prospect* had been published in England

the previous year, had penetrated westward as far as the Concord River. His map contains the first reference to the Musketaquid, or Grass-ground River, at it was called by the Indians. Wood had returned to England in 1633. But there was a man in the Colony who knew the area at first hand.

Simon Willard was not among the first settlers in Boston; he arrived from his home in Kent in the spring of 1634. Apparently he immediately began to explore the back country and the rivers leading to the interior with a view to possible fur trade with the Indians — a business in which John Winthrop and others were already engaged. Soon Willard was promoting the idea of a new town in as promising a spot as could be found east of the Connecticut Valley. It is not easy today, when the original wilderness has been "subdued" to the vanishing point, for us to appreciate how rare and valuable the few naturally open tracts — largely in the river bottoms — must have seemed to men whose very existence depended on grassland for pasturing cattle and plowland for crops. No location was suitable that did not (in the words of one town committee) *"afford boggy meadow or such, that men can live upon."* Even now, if one walks for an hour or two through the Lincoln and Concord woods, emerging, let us say, on the crest of Fairhaven Hill, with its sudden view of the lush valley below, one can recapture the sense of welcome and of hope that such a scene would have evoked three centuries ago. Immediately south lies the swelling in the Sudbury River known as Fairhaven Bay; farther upstream in the same direction begin the Sudbury marshes, where the river meanders through broad meadows of sedge. On the flatland to the north, just above the meeting of the sluggish Sudbury River with the swifter Assabet (Indian for clear or drinking water river) lies the town of Concord. Erasing roads and houses from one's mind, one can see that this was indeed a promising townsite. Not visible from Fairhaven Hill, but known to the future colonists, were other important assets: a brook entering the main river suitable for a milldam, an abundance of marsh grass* for their cattle, and broad fertile levels stretching away to the northeast. Nor was the area lacking in timber: there were many stands of old white pine, of great white oaks, of chestnuts on the hillocks of acid gravel left by the glacier.

Simon Willard, then thirty years old, was a practical and determined man. He took the lead in finding investors and in organizing the petition to the General Court to establish a new town — an enterprise likely to be approved, since it accorded well with Governor Winthrop's policy of expansion. On September 12, 1635, the Court, at its session in New-Town (Cambridge) passed the following Act of Incorporation:

"It is ordered, that there shalbe a plantacon att Musketaquid, & that there shalbe 6 myles of land square to belong to it, & that the inhabitants thereof shall have three yeares imunities from all publ[ic] charges, except traineings; Further, that when any that plant there shall have occacon of carryeing of goods thither, they shall repaire to two of the nexte magistrates where the teames are, whoe shall have power for a yeare to presse draughts, att reasonable rates, to be payde by the owners of the goods, to transport their good thither att seasonable tymes; & the name of the place is changed, & here after to be called Concord."

The sides of the square later turned out to measure nearer six and two-thirds miles each way. Perfect accuracy was neither practical nor necessary; other Massachusetts

---

* The meadow today consists principally of slender, five-foot-high Bent Reed grass (*Calamagrus canadensis*) and the even taller, sturdier Canary grass (*Phalaris arundinacea*) — most likely the same referred to by Francis Higginson: "The grass and weeds grow up to a man's face in the lowlands, and by the rivers abundance of grass and large meadows, without any tree or shrub to hinder the scythe."

grants have added something "for rocks and wasteland."
A certain excess, suggests Concord historian Charles H.
Walcott, may have been allowed for roads and "for slack
in the chain." (The surveyor's equivalent, it would seem,
of the baker's dozen.) A more important question for Concord, and for hundreds of other American towns, is whether
a square is a sensible division of land. Obviously it was the
easiest to lay out. The Puritan settlers liked straight lines
and right angles, and in the case of Concord, way off in the
wilderness, there were no abutters to worry about. (Or so
they thought. Actually they had taken some land claimed
by Watertown, which led to a dispute that was finally settled by creation of the town of Sudbury to the south.) From
the point of view of topography, however, the square is absurd, since it wholly ignores natural features and drainage
patterns. Yet it became the standard method of dividing up
the public domain, as any modern transcontinental traveler
can see from the air. In 1764 Governor Sir Francis Bernard
of Massachusetts urged — apparently without great effect
— that in surveying for new towns, it would be better "in
general to divide them by natural boundaries instead of
imaginary lines." Yet not for another two centuries was
the river basin, unrelated to man-made political divisions,
recognized as the logical unit in land planning.

In any event, Simon Willard, who knew the country at
first hand, made the best of the allotted thirty-six square
miles. He laid his bounds, writes Walcott, "to include six
valuable mill sites, seven natural ponds, more than nine
miles of river, and a large number of smaller streams."
The lines were drawn, and Concord existed — on paper. Before the year was out, it began to exist in fact. We have no
first-hand contemporary account of how these early settlers
got to the Musketaquid. All we have is a high-flown nar-
rative in Edward Johnson's *Wonder-Working Providence*,
written at second hand fifteen years after the event, pictur-

ing them "traveling through unknown woods, and through watery swamps, sometimes passing through the Thickets, where their hands are forced to make way for their bodies passage, and their feete clambering over the crossed Trees, which when they missed they sunke into an uncertaine bottome in water, and wade up to the knees, tumbling sometimes higher and sometimes lower, wearied with this toile, they at end of this meete with a scorching plaine, yet not so plaine, but that the ragged Bushes scratch their legs fouly, even to wearing their stockings to their bare skin in two or three houres . . . In the time of Summer the Sun casts such a reflecting heate from the sweet Ferne, whose scent is very strong so that some herewith have beene very nere fainting, although very able bodies to undergoe much travell, and this not to be indured for one day, but for many, and verily did not the Lord incourage their naturall parts (with hopes of a new and strange discovery, expecting every houre to see some rare sight never seene before) they were never able to hold out, and breake through . . ." A romanticized picture, no doubt, but the fallen trees (there was a hurricane that year), the swamps, and the briars were probably not exaggerated; our woods can provide the same today.

Though we actually know little of the manner of their going, we can make a fair conjecture of the Concord settlers' route. A descendant of one of these first families traced it through early town records and his own knowledge of local topography.* Fortunately for history, the neglect of the streets, which even today makes winter travel in our neighbor city of Cambridge an adventure, has deep roots; as early as 1639 the town of Cambridge was "enjoined to repair her ways . . . leading to Concord; upon pain of five pounds." A hundred and forty years after Concord's founding, on the nineteenth of April, parts of this same

* See *Notes*, p. 250

route would make history; and within two or three generations the final bit of it, where it enters the village, would become famous as a principal seedbed in the "flowering of
New England."

Guided by the previous reconnaissance of Simon Willard
and others, the founders of Concord headed for the most
usable land: the Bedford Levels (as they would come to be
known) where the Indians had their cornfields, and the
meadows bordering the brook, which would soon be
dammed for a mill pond. The first houses were built, facing south, in the shelter of the long ridge running parallel
to the Bay Road.

And what of the Indians, whose cleared fields were a
prime attraction to white settlers hungry for tillable
soil? Musketaquid was one of the principal villages of the
Massachusetts tribe of Algonquians, which was thought to
have once numbered about three thousand.* Before the
white settlers arrived, the plague had reduced it to a few
hundred. This remnant was ruled over by the Squaw
Sachem, widow of a powerful ruler killed in tribal warfare.
The local sachem, Tahattawan, made his home near Nash-
awtuc, "the hill between the rivers," at the junction of
the Sudbury and the Assabet. They practiced a primitive
agriculture, killed game with flint-tipped arrows, found
blueberries on the dry slopes (kept open by burning), and
cranberries in the bog, used weirs to take shad, salmon, ale-
wives, and other fish from the river. By Puritan standards,
they had scarcely "subdued" the land. Now so reduced in
numbers, they were ready to part with it, even the cleared
fields. In 1637 a group of Indians, including Squaw

* Although over a hundred Indian camp sites have been located in the
Concord region, only a few of these were in the area that became Lincoln.
As Richard J. Eaton has written: "There were very few suitable house lots
for them near good fishing and easy farming. Doubtless from their point of
view, our rugged topography of hill, swamp, and rocky forest was only good
for chestnuts, pigeons, turkeys and deer, all of which were within an hour's
lope from their camps along the river.

Sachem and Tahattawan, "did express their consent to the sale of the weire at Concord over against the towne & all the planting ground wch hath bene formerly planted by the Indians, to the inhabitants of Concord . . ."

Payment was made with "hatchets, hoes, knives, cotton cloth and shirts." Note that the English were already firmly settled on the land before these formalities took place. They never doubted their right to it, as subjects of a Christian king. But going through the forms of legal purchase must have given them a double assurance, while at the same time satisfying the former "owners" that they had been given a fair deal.

The Indians along the Musketaquid did not, of course, vanish into the wilderness as soon as they had sold their land. Many of them stuck around the settlement, wandering in and out at will, and clearly the English found this alien presence a strain on their Christian charity. By their standards the Indians were lazy, dirty, and sometimes disorderly. In 1646 Simon Willard and Thomas Flint drew up a list of rules for their conduct with appropriate penalties for each infraction. For picking and eating of lice, the fine was "for every louse a penny." For failing to "weare their haire comely as the English do," four shillings; for murder or adultery, death. They were forbidden to grease themselves, "play at their former games," or enter an Englishman's home without knocking. The penalty for fornication was twenty shillings for the man, but only ten for the woman! As for the prohibition of natural methods of louse control, this seems unrealistic, especially when accompanied by the requirement that the savages be clothed. One Indian woman protested, reasonably enough, that she "had rather go naked than be lousie."

The formalities by which the settlers in Concord obtained title to their land from the Indians, the rules of conduct that they drew up, are part of a larger picture. They

reflect an attitude that could hardly be more different from the American frontier stereotype. The founding of the typical New England town was no haphazard settlement, with every man on his own, but rather a carefully planned use of the land. A site was first chosen for the meeting house and the village green, roads were laid out, and house lots — varying in different communities from a quarter acre to ten acres or more — were established on the green or on nearby streets. The outlying "uplands and meadows" for farming, grazing, and woodlots, were divided into strips and distributed to the settlers by lot — thus one's "lot" was literally that. Common land was of two kinds: the "proprietor's commons," open only to those with proprietory rights, and the "town commons," consisting of land not yet allotted but held for future needs, where pasturage was open to all. Some towns ordered that a certain number of acres of "common field" be set aside for every house lot established.

Such in general was the procedure followed by the founders of Concord, including the area that would later become Lincoln. A model, one might say, for modern town planners who, in setting aside open land for the common use of all, in encouraging "cluster zoning" and in recognizing possible future needs (the "land bank" concept) have come full circle back to principles laid down by our forebears more than three centuries ago.

Of course it was not all so neat and standardized as this might suggest. Procedures varied from town to town depending both on the nature of the terrain and the diverse and sometimes conflicting traditions that individual colonists brought with them from the old country. As any town board member knows too well, town government proceeds by trial and error. It was the objective, the ideal, that was important, then as now. "Each early town was, in a real sense, a little commonwealth," writes Sumner Chilton Powell in his classic study of Sudbury. "Each town could make an attempt to form as much of an ideal state as its leaders could conceive and find agreement on." This is our living heritage. This is the mainstream, however confused by the surface crosscurrents and whirlpools of increasingly complex administration that give direction to today's town government. It underlies the debates at town meeting, the decisions of town boards and committees, the long range plans through which we attempt as best we can to shape our future. No town today, least of all in a suburban area, can or should be a "little commonwealth" independent of the larger community of which it is a part. Yet those social planners who generalize about "suburbia," who would abolish local government in a metropolitan region as an anachronism, might do well to take deeper soundings before they set their course.

Though the towns of early New England employed various methods of distributing their land, the basic principle was the same. Title to all land derived from the English Crown. The largest individual land grants naturally went to the original proprietors or "adventurers" — those who risked their money in the initial venture. Smaller grants were made for "services": to the minister, the schoolteacher, the operator of a sawmill or iron works or printing press, or to a leading citizen in recognition of his services to the town. The tendency from the outset was to avoid accumulation of large estates, which would interfere with the natural growth of the settlements. To this end, purchase and sale of lots generally required town approval. Land speculation, which arose a century later, was virtually unknown at this time. The land was for those who could use it, as Governor Winthrop had made clear in Boston. His policy was "to leave a great part at liberty for newcomers and for commons" — partly to prevent the neglect of trades, partly that "there might be a place to receive such as might come after, seeing that it would be very prejudicial to the commonwealth if men should be forced to go far off for land, while others had much, and could make no use of it other than to please the eye with." Yet despite attempts at regulation, there was a tendency — in the Concord region as elsewhere — for proprietary rights to accumulate in a few hands.

The rulers of the Bay Colony had encouraged planters to settle close together "for safety, Christian communion, schools, civility, and other good ends." How reconcile this

with the fact that a tract six miles square — thirty-six square miles — was considered the best size for a plantation? Early records indicate that such a tract was intended to accommodate sixty families, but that this was not looked upon as the limit of population. And the founding of new communities within this area was anticipated. Did those citizens of Concord, I wonder, who so strongly opposed the founding of Lincoln a century later, recall the words of John Winthrop: "A principal motive which led the court to grant . . . such vast bounds was that when the towns should be increased by their children and servants growing up, etc., they might have place to erect villages where they might be planted, and so the land improved to the more common benefit."

In Concord the original distribution of land was made by the selectmen. This "first division" composed only a small part of the whole grant; the remainder was held in common until the "second division" nineteen years later. The price paid into the Town Treasury was approximately one shilling per acre. At first, in the interests of social unity and compactness — and presumably of safety in the case of Indian troubles — no house lots were assigned more than half a mile from the meetinghouse. Each settler was assigned a strip of arable land, and a strip of upland pasture for his cattle. As Powell has pointed out, these English farmers brought with them to New England two conflicting traditions of land use: on the one hand, the "open field" system, by which plowland, though held individually, was farmed in common; on the other, the East Anglian tradition of individual ownership where each farmer had his own equipment and expected to manage his own land as he saw fit. In Concord, by the very nature of the topography, the second system soon prevailed. To work efficiently, the farmer had to live close to his acres, which generally lay at a distance from the town center. By purchase and by swapping, he consolidated his many small holdings into one large farm on which he built his homestead.

Unhappily, much of the land surrounding the new settlement turned out to be less fertile than anticipated. The sandy soils were poor. The river meadows were subject to summer floods that ruined the hay, and all attempts to drain them by deepening the river channel failed. The pine land afforded "very little feeding for cattel." Cows brought from England became sick from eating acorns. The fields cultivated by the Indians had already lost some of their fertility, and clearing new land was a major undertaking. One tends to think of pioneers as, ipso facto, woodsmen — which these middle-class Englishmen notably were not. Nor were they, by and large, sportsmen skilled in hunting or fishing. Even where wild game was abundant, they were largely dependent on pasture and cropland.

Overworked and disappointed in their hopes, many of the first Concord settlers became restless. Elders sent out from Boston found them "wavering about removal, not finding their plantation answerable to their expectation." Some families returned to England, others decided to move to neighboring towns where conditions appeared to be better. In 1645, when Concord was barely ten years old, a group of citizens petitioned to have their taxes reduced, "the povertie and meannesse of the place we live in not answering the labour bestowed on it." Otherwise, however reluctantly, they would have to leave town. "If it be sayd, wee may go to other places and meete with as many difficulties as here, experience herein satisfies us against many reasons. Such as hardly subsisted with us, and were none of the ablest among us, either for labour or for ordering their occasions, have much thriving in other places they have removed to." In short, the grass looked greener, life easier, elsewhere. "This town was once more populated than it now is," wrote Edward Johnson, at about this time, in his *Wonder-Working Providence*. "Some fainted-hearted soldiers among them, fearing that the land would prove barren, sold their possessions for little and moved to a new plantation . . . The number of families at present are about 50, their buildings are conveniently placed in one straight street under a sunny bank in a low level, their herd of great cattle are about 300."

Meanwhile the General Court had become alarmed at the decline in population of the frontier settlements, which might endanger the whole Colony in case of trouble with the Indians. They passed a restraining order: "In regard of the great danger that Concord, Sudbury and Dedham will be exposed unto, being inland Townes and but thinly peopled, it is ordered that no man now inhabiting and settled in any of the s'd Townes (whether married or single) shall remove to any other Towne without the allowance of the majistrates or the select men of the towns . . ."

The population soon began to recover as new and more productive land was cleared. In 1654 the town voted to make a second division, "to facilitate the equitable distribution of the rest of the land," and assure that farmers had adequate uplands adjoining their meadows. Each owner was given three additional acres for each one he already possessed; the town was to be divided into three "quarters": north, east, and south. Apparently there were as many strong opinions about how this should be done as there would be in Concord or Lincoln today. Then, as now, a committee was appointed. After "much weariness about these things," a detailed plan was accepted, which included woodland set aside for the common use of the town, provisions for the minister and for the poor, and "some inlargement," at the rate of twelvepence per acre, for those "whoe are short in lands." Regulations were set up for the government of each quarter. The parcel that would become the town of Lincoln exactly a hundred years later lay largely in the south quarter. It was following this second division of land that the heirs of Thomas Flint were granted, in recognition of his services to the town, the area we know today as Lincoln Center.

CHAPTER 5 ⌐

"From the earliest foundation of Massachusetts, it was a recognized part of her development that one swarm after another should issue from the hives of the original landings, and seek homes and pasturage on other rivers, other harbors, other plains and hillsides."
-- William Everett, at the dedication of the Lincoln Town House

A Town Is Born

When Governor John Winthrop explained the purpose of the "vast bounds" — the six-mile square — granted to towns such as Concord, he pointed out the need for future villages within them as the population grew. By the time it was a century old, the outlying areas of this growing town were becoming settled to the point where the journey to one central meetinghouse, particularly in winter, was a real hardship. As early as 1734 a group of residents of southeastern Concord and adjacent areas of Lexington and Weston began petitioning their local governments to allow them to establish their own town or precinct. They met with little sympathy. Lexington, which would lose fourteen of its 215 voters and about one eleventh of its acreage, appointed a special committee to oppose the prayer of the petitioners. The committee claimed that many residents of the area were opposed to separation, that some who signed the petition were "very unqualified persons," that the roads were being improved and — this was clearly the main point — they had chosen their minister and they "ought to stay and help pay him." Not surprisingly, the petition was voted down. Concord and Weston reacted the same way, for much the same reasons.

Meanwhile, in Concord, where most of the petitioners lived, some of them at least were becoming unhappy with the religious fare as well as with the effort required to partake of it. The Reverend Daniel Bliss had introduced a new style of preaching: spontaneous, inspirational, enthusiastic. This was the period of the religious revival known as the "Great Awakening." In 1741, Jonathan Edwards, New England's outstanding theologian, preached his famous sermon, "Sinners in the Hands of an Angry God." That same year George Whitefield, the co-founder (with John Wesley) of Methodism, made his first visit to Concord. He and Bliss — both in their mid-twenties — fell into each other's arms. "I preached to some thousands in the open air," wrote Whitefield in his journal, "and comfortable preaching it was. The hearers were sweetly melted down. About £45 was collected for the orphans . . ." He stayed the night with his new friend, that they might rejoice together. Brother Bliss, he records, "broke into floods of tears, and we had reason to cry out it was good for us to be here."

That year fifty joined the church; the following year, sixty-five; in one day alone there were eighteen converts. Thus encouraged, Mr. Bliss seems to have become a true revivalist. "He began in a low, moderate strain," wrote one visitor who heard him, "but toward the close of his sermon, he began to raise his voice and to use many extravagant gestures, and then began a considerable groaning among the auditors, which as soon as he perceived, he raised his voice still higher, and then the congregation were in the utmost confusion, some crying out in the most doleful accents, some howling, some laughing, and others singing, and Mr. Bliss still roaring to them to come to Christ, — they answering, — '*I will, I will, I'm coming, I'm coming.*'" Soon religious meetings were being held throughout the week. And soon Mr. Bliss was in trouble.

Ostensibly, at least, his troubles were less the result of his methods of preaching than of his interpretation of the Word. Such disputes were not unique to Concord, and they bring home to us the extraordinary extent to which not only the church, but the finest points of theological doctrine were in those days a part of daily life, and often the seed of bitter controversy. When enough parishioners became discontented with a minister's performance, a council of ministers from outside would be summoned to take him to task. Such a council had led to the dismissal of Mr. Bliss's predecessor, and now he himself was to be given a thorough working-over. Ministers and delegates from fourteen churches met on September 13, 1743, to examine him and hear his response to twenty-one separate complaints about his faith — particularly his interpretation of the doctrine of "election" — and his conduct of his office. Since he was accustomed to preach extemporaneously, rather than read his sermons, he was at a disadvantage when it came to discussing such nice distinctions as that between being "condemned" and being "damned." Admitting that some of his expressions may have been unfortunate, he nevertheless stuck to his guns in defense of his basic philosophy. "All faith which produceth not good fruits working by love, etc., is accursed and soul-destroying, I have said, and purpose still to say, though some may be offended." Mr. Bliss was admonished but not dismissed. A year later, however, a number of the "most wealthy, respectable, influential, and pious men in town" split off into what was officially called the West Church, but nicknamed The Black Horse Church, from the fact that services were held in the tavern with the sign of the black horse. And a year after that, the residents in the southeasterly part of town who wanted their own meetinghouse and their own preacher at last got their way.

They had been trying for over ten years. In fact, their first petition to the General Court, in 1734, had preceded the trouble over the Reverend Bliss. This petition, which sought permission to establish a new township, was summarily dismissed, as was a similar one the following year.

Most of the petitioners were of course "yeomen" — that is, farmers — but they found a leader for this separatist movement in a man of a different stamp, a wealthy and influential gentleman named Chambers Russell. Descended from a distinguished merchant family, a graduate of Harvard, a lawyer and a judge, married to the granddaughter of Governor Dudley and daughter of Francis Wheelwright, he had settled on his father-in-law's estate, which was part of the original Bulkeley grants lying between Flint's Pond,

Walden Pond, and Fairhaven Bay on the Concord River. He had served as selectman and as Concord's representative in the General Court. Concord records show him active in town affairs, promoting road projects against the opposition of more parsimonious freeholders, giving money for an "Alms or Work House," building a family pew in the meetinghouse to "revert to the Towns use upon the Removal of Sd. Mr. Russel from the Town of Concord or not congregating with Sd. Town." A customary provision, but particularly appropriate in this instance, since Mr. Russell must already have had one eye on a different pew. For some time he had been at odds with his fellow townsmen over their reluctance to run a public way through his estate. Only a separate town would get him his road.

After being turned down again and again by their respective towns, the petitioners in 1744 again went to the General Court, this time for authority to establish a separate precinct. The terms "precinct" and "parish" and "district" were used interchangeably in early colonial statutes. A precinct at this time denoted a definite tract of land; it was a long step toward formation of an independent town. The records of the Court for August 1744 contain "The Petition of the Inhabitants or proprietors of Tenements in the Easterly part of Concord and the Northerly part of Weston and Westerly part of Lexington whose names are unto affixed humbly Sheweth

"That your Petitioners labour under great Difficulties and Inconveniences by reason of their distance from their respective places of publick Worship in said Towns, their Families being many of them Numerous, in the Winter Season more especially, they have been obliged for many years past to promote and Maintain the preaching of the word of God amongst them in a private House, or otherwise many of them must have been deprived of the great Benefit thereof . . . We humbly pray this honorable Court will be pleased to take their case into your wise and serious Consideration, and make them a Precinct, and invest them with such privileges as this honourable court shall see meet . . ."

Not all of the residents in the area joined in the petition; a number of them would continue to belong to the first parish and worship in Concord. But in view of the distances involved, the majority who wanted their own meeting-house can hardly be accused of pampering themselves: "Now many of them live four and some five miles distant from the Places of publick Worship in said Towns; If this petition should be granted there will be but few Inhabitants two miles and a quarter from the Center thereof."

A committee was appointed, hearings were held, and finally on April 24, 1746, the House of Representatives granted the request. A month later the first official precinct meeting — including of course Chambers Russell — was held at the house of Edward Flint, descendant of the Thomas Flint who almost a century before had been granted this corner of Concord in the second division of land. The following year the new congregation united in a Church Covenant, agreeing "to walk together, as a particular church of Christ, according to all those holy rules of the gospel prescribed to such a society so far as we do, or shall, understand the mind of God revealed to us in this respect . . . Likewise give up ourselves one unto another, in the Lord, resolving by his help to cleave to each other, as fellow members of one body, in brotherly love and holy watchfulness over one another . . ."

Even before the General Court had granted their petition for a separate precinct, the future citizens of Lincoln had "prepared a Frame for a Meeting house ready to be set up" and Edward Flint had donated an acre of "clear land" on the south slope of what is now Lincoln Hill. Just a year after its creation, the precinct voted to accept a meetinghouse "already built." This was a plain, unadorned wooden structure, with clapboard sides and shingle roof, almost square, with porches on three sides. Nine years later — at the cost of thirteen pounds, six shillings and eightpence — the town added a steeple with spire at the west end, "to hang a bell upon." Inside, the main body of the building was filled with long benches flanking the central aisle: men sitting on one side, women on the other. A gallery accommodated children, servants, and slaves. Against the walls were built the family pews.

The seating of the meetinghouse was the first order of

business. This was a serious matter, since it publicly proclaimed one's status in the community. Though the New
England town meeting was in many respects a democratic
institution, the church by contrast was firmly hierarchical.
As with Harvard in its early years, precedence was determined by official and social position, and by wealth. On
Lincoln Hill, those "highest in the Valuation for Real Estate" got their first choice of location for their pews — beginning, naturally, with Chambers Russell. Each family
was responsible for building its own pew. Later on, as repairs to the meetinghouse became necessary, the money
was raised by removing some of the benches and selling
new pews to the highest bidders.

It is interesting to note that New Englanders, though
taking the ownership of slaves for granted, nevertheless
could not stomach the idea that a human being was nothing
more than a piece of private property. In authorizing a
committee to seat the meetinghouse, voters of Lincoln stip-
ulated that "age, real and personal estate, slaves excepted,
shall be the rule by which the Committee shall govern
themselves." (A century later Lincoln, along with many
New England towns, voted "that no person who holds or
traffics in slaves shall be admitted to the Communion in this
Church.")

The new precinct was at last a fact, but urgent problems
remained. Committees were set up to survey the precinct
boundaries and to lay out "convenient ways" to the new
meetinghouse — thus establishing the pattern of roads and
dwellings converging on Lincoln Center as we know it today. A "suitable burying place" was provided by Edward
Flint's nephew, Ephraim, who deeded to the town an acre
of land "on a plain between his dwelling house and the
great meadow" — for which act of generosity the town
built him a pew at public expense. Now the principal concern was to employ "some meet Person to preach the word

of God." A search committee eventually invited a twenty-five-year-old schoolteacher named William Lawrence to preach on probation for four Sundays. He having been found suitable, Chambers Russell was delegated to treat with him in respect to his salary — in cash and in firewood. (The former included a cost-of-living provision based on current prices of four staple commodities of colonial New England: Indian corn, rye, beef, and pork.) Young Lawrence, son of a Groton farmer, had "persuaded my Father to put me to Learning and Send me to Colledge"; he graduated from Harvard at the age of fifteen. As a preacher, he appears to have been more industrious than inspiring, grinding out an average of seventy sermons a year, which showed "a careful exegesis, a calm logical method, an earnest purpose, a somewhat conventional style." There was "no allusion to passing events." In fact, the only time that Lawrence got into trouble with his congregation was when he failed actively to support the Revolutionary War. [See Notes, p. 000.] He and his wife, named Love, lived in "a low-studded two story building — a modest abode, with whitewashed walls and sanded floors and plain furniture. The parlor contained a mahogany table, a walnut desk, a little round tea-table, six leathern-seated chairs, a few books of divinity, and the family Bible." However, there seems to have been room for a slave. He notes in his diary for 1778: "Dyed Cumbo, a negro woman living in my house, and leaft to Mrs. Lawrence by her mother at her death." And by the end of his life he owned more than seventy acres of land in town, including "a good farm of thirty-nine acres connected with the homestead," extending from the crest of Lincoln Hill all the way to Flint's Pond. Tradition relates that when one of his parishioners jokingly asked him how he managed to get on so well, he replied, "By minding my own business, and letting yours alone."

Though the future citizens of Lincoln had their meeting-

house and their pastor, they were only partway to their
goal. Within a year of its founding, the second precinct, as
it came to be called, had expressed its desire "to be made
into a Distinct Township." Again and again the request
was refused. The final attempt to win local approval, to
achieve independence with the blessing of the mother
town, was made at Concord's annual town meeting of
March 4, 1754. "*Article 4:* To See if the Town will Sett off
those Inhabitants of Concord that live Within the Bounds
of the New precinct in the Easterly part of Said Town in
Order to be Joyned with others of Lexington and Weston
to be erected into a Separate Township or District as the
General Court Shall see Meet agreeable to the Request of
Mr. Edward Flint and Others." There followed a long, and
no doubt heated, discussion, with each side presenting arguments that by then were painfully familiar: the petitioners
impatient to move on from partial to complete autonomy,
their fellow townsmen concerned with the loss of tax revenue that this would involve. Then as now, the opposition
was quick to take advantage of any vagueness or incon-
sistency in the presentation of the article. Surprisingly, in
view of the length of time they had been at it, Flint and his
neighbors seem to have failed to define the exact area the
new town would encompass, and also failed to present their
case as clearly as they might. Or perhaps their opponents
were merely seizing on this as an excuse. At last it came to
a vote. "The Request of Mr. Edward Flint and others being
Read and fully Debated and it appearing that there was an
uncertainty in the Bounds mentioned in said Request and
the Request and Explaination of the same by the petitions
[petitioners] appearing so different and not easily to be understood, Therefore noted that the fourth Article which relates to the Same be passed over."*

* The fact that the future town of Carlisle, then northern Concord, was in
process of becoming a separate District must have increased the Concord
voters' concern.

Once more, the only recourse was an appeal to the General Court. The time was not propitious, since during this period Governor William Shirley was discouraging the founding of new towns: the more Representatives there were to the General Court, the harder it would be for the Royal Governors to control it. But the Russell family had great influence; Chambers' father sat on the Governor's Council, his brother in the House of Representatives. And the Governor had been temporarily back in England. When he returned, he quarreled with the Legislature over his salary, and had no mind to strain relations further by opposing it in other matters. Chambers Russell saw his chance and pushed the measure through ahead of schedule. The petition for a separate township was presented to the Great and General Court on March 28, 1754. It had three readings within ten days and went to the Governor on April 19.

A week earlier, a committee appointed by the Concord selectmen, in a last-ditch attempt to block this division of their town, had appealed directly to Governor Shirley. They claimed, in essence, that the desire for separation was by no means unanimous and that the complaint about distance from the Concord meetinghouse was nonsense. "Their Great Difficulties they Pretend to be under on account of Roads your Respondants apprehend are without foundation, and the facts asserted we do not understand; the Selectmen of Concord having laid out several ways to their desire . . ." What is more, Concord had paid for these roads, which would now belong to another town. And with so many taxpayers taken off the rolls, how could the citizens of Concord take care of their poor, or maintain their bridges? "Other reasons might be given were it not for the shortness of the time allowed . . ."

All in vain. On April 23, the Governor reluctantly signed the bill creating the new town, which then included 690 persons. In recognition of his valiant service as midwife,

Judge Russell was given the privilege of christening the newborn child. He chose to name it Lincoln, after Lincolnshire, England, the birthplace of his grandfather, Charles Chambers. The choice was most appropriate. "Lincolnshire," in the words of Thomas Hutchinson, "contributed greatly, and more of our principal families derive their origin from thence than from any part of England, unless the city of London be an exception."

On April 26, 1754, the citizens of Lincoln held their first town meeting.

CHAPTER 6 ⌉

"Our own American past has an invaluable lesson to teach us:
a coherent, workable landscape evolves where there is a coherent
definition not of man but of man's relation to the world and to his
fellow men."
— John Brinckerhoff Jackson, *Jefferson, Thoreau and After*

A Way of Life

Boston, some observers have suggested, is a state of mind. The small New England town, however, may be better described as a way of life. Obviously this is no longer so true as it was two centuries ago; in a modern suburb, as distinguished from a country village, the very idea may seem far-fetched. Yet the fact is that towns, like men, have their characters formed in their youth. They may grow old and die, like the ghost towns of the gold rush, when the reason for their existence has come to an end. Or, if near big cities, they may die a different sort of death, not of starvation but of glut. Those that do survive, however, will have their own distinct personalities, based on their past. They will endure as communities with whom men and women can identify themselves, communities with ingrained attitudes established over many generations. Such attitudes are tough to eradicate, even in the name of what may, at the moment, be defined as progress. Fortunately, definitions change. Standards of value traditionally associated with rural New England no longer look as quaint as they did a generation ago. Though few Lincoln residents would willingly change places with their predecessors, the way these people lived and thought will always be an element in the character of the town.

Composed as it was of outlying districts of three existing

towns, Lincoln not only began as an agricultural community, but remained so well into the present century. It was founded at a time when, according to modern historians, the New England town was reaching its highest state of development in terms of a harmonious relation between man and the land. This was also the time when European intellectuals, preaching the doctrine of the simple life, were coming to look upon the husbandman as the ideal citizen: a concept popularized by Thomas Jefferson and still a part of the American credo. Jefferson's dream was that of a democratic society of small independent landowners; to him "those who labor in the earth are the chosen people of God. . . whose breasts he has made his peculiar deposit for substantial and genuine virtue."

None of these lofty considerations, had he known them, would likely have turned the head of the Yankee farmer, who had no choice but to make a virtue of the hard life. An individualist, he was also a good neighbor by inclination as well as by necessity. While believing in the "work ethic," he made every communal event — a barn-raising, a funeral, and especially the weekly Sabbath service — an occasion for sociability. He was wedded to the soil in a way that we can never know, for the land was his immediate source of life. Moreover, its possession, free and clear of claims by any overlord, was a symbol of his personal dignity and independence. "The instant I enter on my own land," wrote St. John Crèvecoeur in *Letters from an American Farmer*, "the bright idea of property, of exclusive right, of independence exalt my mind . . . No wonder that so many Europeans who have never been able to say that such a portion of land was theirs, cross the Atlantic to realize that happiness." Land was a family treasure to be cherished and parceled out, as contemporary deeds and wills bear witness, with meticulous care. It was also a public responsibility, the administration of which gave the townsman essential training for practical politics. Without such local experience, he could never have coped with the broader and far more complex problems that would be involved in the founding of a new nation.

Surviving inventories help us to imagine the physical character of the landscape as it appeared two centuries ago and to recognize the forces that shaped it. When Lincoln was thirty years old, it contained eighty-eight dwellings, and no fewer than eighty-four barns. About two fifths of the area of the town was open land. Over a third of this was pasturage. Next in extent came the "fresh meadow" or native grassland. (Presumably low wetlands kept open by periodic controlled flooding.) Finally, and most valuable, were the smaller areas given over to "English mowing," planted with seed imported from abroad, and the "tillage" or cultivated land devoted to the raising of food crops. In the early days of the Colony the principal crop was of course Indian corn, or maize, one variety of which was similar to the multicolored ears used today for decorations at Thanksgiving time. "In the pure Northerly parts," wrote John Winthrop, Jr., of Connecticut, "they have a peculiar kind called Mohawks corn, which though planted in *June*, will be ripe in season. The stalks of this kind are shorter, and the Ears grow nearer the bottom of the stalk, and are generally of divers colours." Corn meal provided the staple diet, along with pumpkins, beans, and peas — the last two often planted alongside the corn whose stalks served for beanpoles. Wheat, with which the colonists were familiar at home, was soon introduced but was successful only in the more fertile areas and was subject to blight; rye was sturdier and better suited to light and gravelly soils. Barley was grown for the making of beer (the favorite drink before cider came into production) and oats for the horses.

"Gardens were literally of the first importance to the early settlers of New England," writes Ann Leighton in her

charming and definitive *Early American Gardens*. "Too
sensible to expect to be fed by either the natives or the
never-failing lushness of tropical lands, they knew from
early explorers' tales that they would have to grow their
own food as soon as their ships' stores ran out." She quotes
some verses written by Governor Bradford of the Plymouth
Plantation which show that, while vegetables and herbs
were necessities for survival, flowers also had their place in
the garden from the very beginning:

> All sorts of roots and herbes in gardens grow,
> Parsnips, carrots, turnips, or what you'll sow,
> Onions, melons, cucumbers, radishes,
> Skirrets, beets, coleworts, and fair cabbages.
> Here grow fine flowers many and mongst those,
> The fair white lily and sweet fragrant rose.

As the land was cleared and settled, the vegetable garden
became a part of every home and the diet of the New England farmer achieved a considerable variety. Here is a
recollection of one such garden as it must have been at the
end of the colonial period: "a wilderness of onions, squashes,
cucumbers, beets, parsnips and currants, with the never-
failing tansey for bitters, horseradish for seasoning, and
fennel for keeping old women awake in church time."

Returning to the Lincoln inventory, we find that woodland, comprising three fifths of the total, was divided
into two almost equal categories: "improved" and "unim-
proved." A small residue — which must have been really
rough — is described in the town records with apparent
resignation as "unimprovable."

Soil conditions varied greatly in different parts of the
town. "Lincoln has all the varieties of soil, from the richest
to the poorest," writes an early nineteenth century historian. "Though rough and uneven, it contains some of the
best farms in the county." The Lincoln farmer by the

time of the Revolution was cultivating, on the average, about six acres of land: the amount that could be efficiently worked with one pair of oxen. Ephraim Hartwell had 20 acres of "tillage," but that was the largest tract in town. More typically, Thomas Brooks and his son Noah together held 10 acres of tillage, 28 of mowing and 32 of pasture. The inventory of the estate of Jabez Stratton, a farmer and mill owner who died when Lincoln was a week old, estimates his land at 75 acres. His "quick stock" consisted of "one grizld cow, one red Ditto, lyned back cow, Brown cow, one pair oxen, one Horse, one pair stears, one heifer, two yearling stears, one sow, two barrows [castrated pigs]." Altogether the town provided pasturage and hay for over 300 cows, for about 100 horses and half again as many oxen. Most farmers raised sheep and of course pigs. Goats, which were shipped over in quantity when the Bay Colony was founded, seem largely to have disappeared. This was a blessing, since they are the greatest enemies of the land, as anyone who visits a country like Greece can clearly see today.

Next to its stone walls, perhaps the most characteristic and most beautiful feature of the cultivated New England landscape was its apple orchards. Their extent can be judged by the fact that, in the Revolutionary period, Lincoln farmers were annually pressing some 800 barrels of cider, not to mention the variety of apples which, by drying or winter storage, could be eaten throughout much of the year, and even exported. "There is no farmer, or even cottager, without a large orchard," wrote the anonymous author of *American Husbandry* in 1775, "some of them of such extent, that they make three or four hundred hogsheads of cyder a man [Lincoln's figures look modest by comparison!] besides exporting immense quantities of apples from all parts of the province." John Adams, according to his descendant Charles Francis Adams, drank a tankard of hard cider every morning before breakfast. When James Barrett of Concord made his will, the provision for his wife included four barrels of cider a year, or about three pints a day. As the winter wore on, cider stored in the cellar gathered strength; if a man acted a bit frisky, it would be remarked that his cider was getting hard. And when the temperance movement eventually seized hold of the country in the mid-nineteenth century, whole orchards were cut down with misdirected zeal on the assumption that hard cider was their only product.

With its well-kept orchards and fields of waving grain, its rolling pastures and lush level grasslands, the landscape of New England had, by the late colonial period, become civilized to the point where visitors from Old England felt at home. The redcoats who would soon be marching on Concord would find it rough and hostile, with its thickets and stone walls so well suited to guerrilla warfare, but there was also much open country, kept so not for aesthetic reasons but because the most important single crop was grass. "A large portion of every farm in New England," continues *American Husbandry*, "consists of meadow and pasture land; wherein it much resembles the better parts of the mother country. In the low lands, the meadows are rich, yielding large quantities of hay, which, though apparently coarse, is yet much liked by all cattle; the common herbage of many of these is a grass which has made much noise in England under the name of Timothy grass." As we have seen, it was the native grasslands that first lured settlers to the site of Concord. The corner which, together with bits of Lexington and Weston, was to become Lincoln had no such extensive water meadows, but a surprising proportion of it is natural swamp and bog, as the early farmers knew and as recent sophisticated studies have demonstrated in the course of mapping the town for wetland zoning. Where open meadow did not exist it could be created and maintained by artificial means. Talking with old-timers, one sometimes realizes with a shock how much our local landscape has changed. East of my house lies a long belt of swampland down the center of which flows a sluggish brook or ditch; the muck is deep and walking is best when the ground is frozen. Today it is covered with a dense growth of hardwoods. But an elderly neighbor recalled a conversation many years ago with a farmer who, as a boy, had carried jugs of drinking water to the men who were cutting hay on this very spot.

Remains of dams and drainage ditches all over town remind us of how farmers in bygone days used to flood such areas every year to keep the trees from coming back, and then drain them to allow the grass to grow. Evidently they brought this technique with them from England; the diary of Adam Winthrop, John's father, refers to "drowning the meadow." So with the cranberries. Close by that swamp which was once an open field lies a small cranberry bog that has generally yielded enough berries for our children to make Thanksgiving jelly. It is one of more than a dozen abandoned bogs that have been harvested within the memory of Lincoln residents. Most are now grown up to woods, indicating that they, like the grasslands, had to be managed in order to survive. The wetlands also determined the pattern of our town roads. By necessity, roads followed the high ground, as did the historic highway from Lexington to Concord; this was before the days when roadways were cut and filled regardless of the contours of the land.

If Europeans found the New England scene familiar and therefore pleasing, it was not because of any conscious effort on the part of her citizens. It was rather the result of a way of life. Wise and thrifty use of land had produced a beautiful landscape, as it had generations earlier in the English rural villages, the hill towns of Italy, or the terraced gardens of Japan. The very spareness of the soil, the scarcity of usable land, meant that the farmer thought in terms of living *with* his land, not simply living *off* it. From the beginning its possession was his pride, a symbol as well as a livelihood. "The generation which planned the New England villages, divided the fields, and built the first houses, seemed incapable of making anything ugly," writes Professor Morison. "If their laying out of homestead, village common, stone wall, road, meeting-house was unconscious, the more to the credit of their instinct; for it was done in harmony with the lay of the land, the contours of valley and slope, the curve of stream and shore."

Neither fields nor village, of course, took shape overnight. It must have been years before the rotting stumps were cleared from the village green, and generations before the dooryard elms — though they are fast-growing trees — reached their full grandeur. Nor were these early villages so manicured and pretty as later reconstructions and lifeless imitations might lead one to believe. The colonial cottage, white with green shutters, set off by a neat lawn surrounded with a picket fence, never existed outside the real estate advertisements. Before 1800 few houses were painted (except possibly the trim) though some were stained red or green. A typical house of the Revolutionary period was, in the memoirs of one who knew it, of "dun complexion assumed by unpainted wood, exposed to the weather for twenty or thirty years, save only that the roof was tinged a reddish-brown by a fine moss that found sustenance in the chestnut shingles."* No lawn; just a split-rail fence to keep out the cows. Nor did the house front on a tree-lined street; that too was a development of the nineteenth century. Virtually every house had its barn; today the few that remain are priceless treasures. Crèvecoeur, writing at this same time, remarks that the barn "is an object, in the mind of the farmer, superior even to his dwelling. Many don't care much how they are lodged, provided they have a good barn and barn-yard."

Obviously the farmer in Concord or Lincoln, in contrast to his brother in Boston, was dependent for his daily fare on the produce of his own acres. With their continual reference to salt beef and salt pork, to corn and rye, early documents would suggest a certain monotony of diet. But these were just the staples. As the garden described above bears witness, early New Englanders enjoyed a variety of vegetables, and even seventeenth-century descriptions include a great many fruits and berries. Wild game was abundant at the beginning, but soon declined; that magnificent symbol of Puritan New England, the wild turkey (a bronze-tailed bird far more beautiful than his domestic English cousin) had all but disappeared by the end of the seventeenth century. The principal game bird, to be reduced by man's greed from unbelievable abundance to extinction, was of course the passenger pigeon. "The cheapest of all the several kinds of poultry," recounts a visitor to Boston in 1740, "are a sort of wild pigeon, which are in season the latter end of June, and so continue until September. They are large, and finer than those we have in London, and are sold here for eighteen-pence a dozen, and sometimes for half of

---

* In 1858 Henry Thoreau wrote in his journal: "In the hazy atmosphere yesterday we could hardly see Garfield's old unpainted farmhouse. It was only betrayed by its elms. This would be the right color for painters to imitate."

that." Lincoln took its own small part in the infamous slaughter of the passenger pigeon. In the account books of Lincoln merchant Joshua Child, we find this entry: July 2, 1776 — "To Neting a Pigeon Net* 2.10.0." And in a corner of my woods there is a small rise known as Pigeon Hill. Once it was shaded by great oaks; here huge flocks of these lovely birds would stop to roost on migration, the branches bending under the weight of their numbers. All that now remains of their passage is their name.

The incredible numbers of so-called "game birds" vanished with the wilderness, in New England as elsewhere throughout America. The Puritans doubtless considered this a loss, since they were worth eating. As to other species, I doubt that they or their descendants were aware that, by opening up the forest, by creating meadows and orchards and forest edge, they were providing a variety of habitat that greatly increased the abundance of songbirds: bobolinks and meadowlarks in the fields, orioles and bluebirds in the orchards, warblers darting among the treetops, swallows and flycatchers snatching insects from the air. Whether the farmer recognized it or not, these insect-eaters were his friends. He had no trouble, however, in recognizing his enemies: the grain-eaters that descended on his crops. Concord was not long in urging upon her Selectmen "that incorigment be given for the destroying of blackbirds and jaies." A century later Lincoln, by then an independent town, followed suit, and established a bounty "to encourage and bring forward the destruction of those mischievous birds called the Black Bird and the Crow,"

---

* St. John Crèvecoeur, in his *Letters from an American Farmer*, 1782, gives a rather sickening description of how the net was sometimes used. "We catch them with a net extended on the ground, to which they are allured by what we call *tame wild pigeons*, made blind, and fastened to a long string; his short flights, and his repeated calls, never fail to bring them down. The greatest number I ever catched was fourteen dozen, though much larger quantities have often been trapped. I have frequently seen them at the market so cheap, that for a penny you might have as many as you could carry away."

with the macabre provision that sixpence be paid "for each Crow that is feathered and three pence for each young Crow not feathered." In 1818 the state legislature passed an act prohibiting the killing of birds, but providing for suspension of the act by town governments. Regularly Lincoln voted "to kill Birds as usual." Nevertheless the crows and blackbirds and jays, unlike the turkeys and passenger pigeons, have conspicuously held their own as a permanent part of our rural landscape. "What a perfectly New England sound," writes Thoreau, "is the voice of the crow! . . . This bird sees the white man come and the Indian withdraw, but it withdraws not. Its untamed voice is still heard above the tinkling of the forge . . . It remains to remind us of aboriginal nature."

The great mammals have not fared so well. Thoreau keenly felt their loss. "When I consider that the nobler animals have been exterminated here — the cougar, panther, lynx, wolverine, wolf, bear, moose, deer, beaver, the turkey, etc., etc., — I cannot but feel as if I lived in a tamed, and, as it were, emasculated country. . . As if I were to study a tribe of Indians that had lost all its warriors." He was wrong, however, about the white-tailed deer. Though by the early eighteenth century it had been so reduced in Massachusetts that a closed season was established — enforced by wardens or "deer reeves" — it recovered spectacularly in the cut-over forest, since it flourishes on low, tender new growth. Today the problem is one of overpopulation, for the other "noble animals" that once kept it in check are no more.

*   *   *

No community can live by farming alone, least of all a colony three thousand miles from the mother country. The New England town, like the English country manor, had to be in most respects self-sufficient, with its own industries and trades. As early as 1658, a company was incorporated "to erect one or more iron-works in Concord," to exploit the local-bog iron ore. Lime was quarried in several parts of town. Remains of two such quarries can still be seen in Lincoln, and in Concord's Estabrook Woods are the foundations of a lime kiln, mentioned in Thoreau's Journal. Like Thoreau, we may "read a new page in the history of these parts in the old limestone quarries and kilns where the old settlers found the materials of their houses." Bricks soon replaced daub and wattle in construction of chimneys; long before Lincoln separated from Concord, a brickyard was operating in what is now the northwest corner of town. Lincoln like other villages had its own masons and carpenters, its blacksmiths and coopers, its rope makers and cordwainers (shoe and saddle makers), its sawmills and gristmills and, close by the brickyard, a prosperous tannery operated by one of the leading families. It had its local weavers and dyers (such as Joshua Child, who sold the pigeon nets); there is also a reference in the town records to a "woolen factory," where presumably spinning, carding, and fulling were carried on. In the early eighteenth century there was also a glassworks on the crest of Lincoln Hill.

One tends to think of the Puritans as dressed in sober black and white. Actually they loved color, and they found dyes for their woolens close at hand: brown and yellows from red oak or hickory bark, crimson from the juice of the pokeberry, orange from the sassafras, purple from the iris. And by the end of the seventeenth century they had indigo from Barbados — a deep blue which, mixed with goldenrod and alum, also provided a beautiful green. The gentry, of course, imported fine clothes from England: silk and lace, gold and silver thread, ruffs and ribbons and "other superfluous trimmings" in the words of an early statute forbidding the wearing of such finery to all but the rich and wellborn. It was not, in any case, likely to be seen in Lincoln, a town of yeomen and artisans who dressed in homespun.

A Lincoln inventory just before the Revolution lists nine "work Houses" as distinguished from "dwelling Houses." We get a broader picture of industry throughout the Concord–Lincoln region in the detailed list of manufactures compiled during the war in a futile attempt to hold down prices. They include tow cloth and cotton cloth and woolens, felt hats and "Good yarn Hose for men," shoes and saddles, pots and pans, and charcoal at 10 shillings the basket. In the years following independence, Concord developed into a considerable manufacturing center. Here were produced iron and steel, lead pipe, guns, "brass time pieces," lumber, boots, hats, and many other commodities for export. A cotton mill was built as early as 1805. Among later products were the famous lead pencils whose manufacture Thoreau briefly carried on with something less than enthusiasm. He was "put to it to raise the wind to pay for *A Week on the Concord and Merrimack Rivers.* I was obliged to manufacture a thousand dollars' worth of pencils and slowly dispose of and finally sacrifice them, in order to pay an assumed debt of a hundred dollars."*

Though Lincoln did have some export industry — including in later years a glassworks and a pickle factory — it remained, in comparison with its mother town, a rural community, bound to the rhythm of the seasons. In winter, ice was cut on Flint's Pond.** As the sap began to rise, the maple trees were tapped for sugar. Corn was planted when

---

* A month earlier, Thoreau had noted in his *Journal:* "For a year or two past, my *publisher,* falsely so called, has been writing . . . to ask what disposition should be made of the copies of *A Week on the Concord and Merrimack Rivers* still on hand . . . 706 copies of an edition of 1000 which I bought of Munroe four years ago and have been ever since paying for, and have not quite paid for yet. . . So I had them all sent to me here. . . I have now a library of nearly nine hundred volumes, over seven hundred of which I wrote myself. Is it not well that the author should behold the fruits of his labor?"

** This pond was also considered "a favorite resort for pickerel." Fishing through the ice became so popular that in 1824 the legislature passed an act prohibiting any person, under penalty of two dollars, from fishing "with more than one hook" between December 1 and April 1.

the woods awoke in the pastel colors of spring and the bud-
ding oak leaves had reached the size of a mouse's ear. The
first hay crop was harvested in June; blueberries ripened in
July and corn in August; cranberries in the bogs and apples
on the hillside orchards grew red as summer turned into
fall. With them came what Thoreau called the greatest
crop of all, the falling leaves. "This, more than any mere
grain or seed, is the great harvest of the year. . . I am more
interested in it than in the English grass alone or in the
corn. It prepares the virgin mould for future cornfields on
which the earth fattens. They teach us how to die."

Once the land has been settled, farming communities
tend to grow slowly. When it was founded in 1754, Lincoln
had a population of 690. Fifty years later the figure was
750 — a growth rate of approximately one person per year.
In 1904, the hundred and fiftieth anniversary, there were
still only about 1100 people living on fifteen square miles
— almost eight acres for each resident. Unlike its parent
town, Lincoln did not begin with the compact pattern of the
colonial "nuclear village." Yet there was a nucleus, older
than the town itself. As we have seen, even before Lincoln
became a precinct its confident and handy inhabitants had
framed their meetinghouse on the slopes of Lincoln Hill.

The church was of course the unifying force in the settlement of New England. Here, in the words of John Cotton,
was to be a "Garden of the Saints," hedged in from the untamed wilderness — a concept that fostered both brotherly
love and unbrotherly intolerance. This religious fervor
cooled off with the decline of the Puritan movement (to be
temporarily warmed over during the Great Awakening, by
such revivalists as the Reverend Mr. Bliss of Concord). "In
the social rather than the theological sphere," writes Carl
Bridenbaugh, "lies the lasting significance of the New England churches."

Throughout New England the meetinghouse or "House

of Worship" — the building itself was never called a church — was for many generations a principal focus of social as well as spiritual life. The typical colonial farmhouse, with its small rooms surrounding a central chimney, was not designed for large-scale social entertaining; the parlor was reserved for such ceremonial occasions as family prayers and the entertainment of important callers. The meeting-house served the purpose of a "superparlor" (to use J. B. Jackson's metaphor), where the "superfamily" or church congregation met at least once or twice a week. There were two long services on the Sabbath; the "nooning" or "horse-shedding" during the intermission, when friends would adjourn to the horse sheds for gossip, was the social event of the week. In colonial times, churchgoing could be a rugged business. In winter it involved not only riding or driving or tramping through the snow but also sitting out the in-terminable sermons in freezing cold with one eye on heaven and the other on the sand in the hourglass that was placed in the pulpit. Samuel Sewall records in his diary "an Extraordinary Cold Storm of Wind and Snow. Bread was frozen at Lords Table." Not till early in the nineteenth century did meetinghouses begin to be heated; Lincoln installed a wood stove in 1827.

Yet apparently in the absence of other diversion or cultural gatherings, church was considered to be fun. It provided an occasion for singing in a society that generally eschewed music as vanity. Sermons were expertly criticized* and preachers held to a high professional standard of learning and use of language which would make many a minister today quake in his pulpit. By the same token, parishioners had to show them respect. In Concord, John Hoar was fined ten pounds in 1668 for describing the minister's blessing of the congregation as "no better than vain

---

* See Eleazer Brooks's correspondence with the Reverend William Lawrence, p. 122

babbling." A century later, a villager in Connecticut had to make a public apology for remarking that "I would rather hear my dog bark than Mr. Billings preach."

The younger members of the congregation may have attended less closely to the sermon, but there were other attractions. On a lucky day, a dog might elude the tithing-men posted at the meetinghouse doors and disrupt the service. More mature pleasures are suggested by the reprimand delivered to a youth in the venerable town of Ipswich for "taking of the maids by the aprons as they came into the meeting house . . . putting his hand on their bosoms."

Solemnity and sociability were not incompatible. The funeral of Lincoln's first minister, William Lawrence, was observed with pomp and feasting; colleagues and friends of the deceased came from afar to join his parishioners in generous tribute, the dimensions of which can be envisaged from items listed in the town records. They included 500 pounds of English hay (for the visitors' horses); quantities of veal, pork, butter, and cheese; both Indian and rye meal, with "3 women to cook." Solace was provided by a barrel of cider, a gallon of wine, and a gallon of rum. The installation of Dr. Lawrence's successor, Charles Stearns, was more liberally supplied with drink, as befitted a joyous occasion: 9 gallons of wine and 5 gallons of rum, along with tea, coffee, chocolate, spices, pipes and tobacco.

Early New England ministers were anything but puritanical when it came to drinking. John Winthrop had scarcely set foot on these shores when he wrote to a friend in England about the possibility of making a "good harde wine" from the local grapes. The Reverend Ezra Ripley, successor to William Emerson in the Concord pulpit, waxed indignant if rum were lacking at a funeral where he presided. His personal household accounts were consistent with his public position. For a single month they ran thus: "1 gal. N.E. rum, 1 gal. wine, 1 gal. W.I. rum, 2 lbs. coffee." Similarly, the charge accounts of Dr. Lawrence with Lincoln's Joshua Child indicate that he bought rum by the gallon, accompanied by an equal quantity of molasses. Edwin M. Stearns, Dr. Charles Stearns's grandson, recalled at the time of the hundred-and-fiftieth anniversary: "As a rule, those old-time reverend gentlemen seldom undertook to preach a sermon without their preliminary toddy. Indeed, it was considered such a necessity that when my father commenced preaching my mother received the following injunction from Grandmother Stearns, viz., 'Betsey, never allow Daniel to go into the pulpit until he has had his rum.' "

Liquor and feasting aside, the ordination of Charles Stearns as Lincoln's second pastor was, in retrospect, an occasion for rejoicing in a deeper sense than anyone could have appreciated at the time. Here is not the place to recount the history of Lincoln's First Parish; that has been published elsewhere, and is largely of local interest. But the career of Dr. Stearns has special significance in showing how the personal qualities of a minister could, over a long period, reflect — and to some extent shape — the character of a town.

Descendant of one of the first settlers in Watertown, Charles Stearns was a fifth-generation New Englander. When Lincoln called him to its church, after the customary trial sermons, he was twenty-eight years old: a Harvard graduate, a student of divinity, a literary man distinguished enough to be appointed a Harvard Tutor. The leading citizens of Lincoln, concerned with their children's education, soon realized their good luck. They founded a "Liberal School" with Dr. Stearns as the preceptor. He loved teaching and needed the extra money. Here he prepared more than forty Lincoln boys for Harvard, at the same time publishing textbooks and "dramatic dialogues," in which virtue and vice fought it out in unmistakable terms, for the moral instruction of the young. When he had reached middle age and was firmly planted in his pulpit, he even went so far as to publish a long poem he had written as a college undergraduate, entitled *The Ladies' Philosophy of Love*, to show "the accomplishments of women as amiable objects [and] the means by which they keep men's affections." "Since that time," he wrote in the preface, "the writer has been a lover — a husband — a father of a numerous family — a pastor — a preceptor for many years to youth of both sexes. His experience has not disproved, but confirmed his principles." By then he was a portly gentleman, "thought to bear a resemblance to Dr. Samuel Johnson in physique, in his peremptory manner, and in his fondness for tea." Oliver Wendell Holmes recalls him in *The Poet at the Breakfast-Table* as the "bulky Charles Stearns of Lincoln . . . How I stared at him! He was the first living person ever pointed out to me as a poet."

In his biographical sketch (from which much of the above is drawn) the Reverend Edward G. Porter writes: "With such a deep interest in poetry, music, philosophy, and religion, Mr. Stearns readily commanded the admiration of his people. He led them into new paths of thought and feeling. . . He helped to make life on these farms less commonplace and more inspiring. He was a teacher as well as preacher; and the forty young men whom he fitted for college. . . were the best proof of his success. . . He gave tone to society." He also held the Lincoln congregation together for the forty-five years of his pastorate, steering a middle course between Congregationalism and the new Unitarianism which was causing schisms elsewhere. Stearns abhorred sectarian disputes; one can almost hear him snort with impatience over petty quarrels on points of dogma. There were, however, already some defections from his congregation before he died; under his successors, the Lincoln church, like so many others, split in two, not to be reunited for exactly a century.

Dr. Stearns's reputation reached beyond the borders of Lincoln. Scholars respected him; he was elected a Fellow of the American Academy of Arts and Sciences the same year as William Ellery Channing, when John Adams was president of the Academy. He exchanged pulpits with his learned brethren in Cambridge and elsewhere. He was even approached as a possible candidate for the presidency of Harvard. He declined to be considered; he could not afford it, and anyway he was content where he was. His flock was content also. When at length he went to his reward, a long eulogy inscribed on his tombstone near the meetinghouse included these words: "By his piety, benevolence and learning he gained the affection and respect of his beloved people. . ." In turn, he left his stamp upon them and upon their town.

Trial by Fire

CHAPTER 7 ⌐

"By the rude bridge that arched the flood,
   "Their flag to April's breeze unfurled
"Here once the embattled farmers stood
   "And fired the shot heard round the world."
— Ralph Waldo Emerson, *Concord Hymn*

"I who know less than nothing about American history, always
find that these early days have a sort of shining quality about
them that is almost Greek. Like the siege of Troy, which must have
been really a very small affair, small episodes, easy to grasp,
have world-wide, almost eternal importance."
— Letter from Georgina Battiscombe, Windsor, England, 1975

Embattled Farmers

Often it is the small accidents of daily living rather than the monuments and museums that bring history alive. Not so long ago Lincoln's Cemetery Commissioner — who was also the grave digger — was preparing a place for another occupant of a family plot in the old town cemetery. His spade struck hard against some bones — no coffin, just bones. Mingled with them were brass buttons and bits of red cloth. Not being an historian, he shoveled them aside and went on with his job. Whoever provided the British "lobsterbacks" with their uniforms had used good cloth and a fast dye; it had endured in the earth since April 20, 1775. The events of the previous day have not only endured but have become a symbol of what America once stood for: the right of a people to govern themselves, the courage and endurance of a small nation faced with sheer military might from abroad.

Though New England town meetings came to be termed "hotbeds of sedition" by the British authorities, there is no hint of the coming troubles in the record of the first decade of Lincoln's own independence as a town. "The proceedings of the town appear to have been conducted with harmony," writes Lemuel Shattuck (which is merely to say that no quarrels were officially recorded). "No occurrence worthy of notice marks its history till the great question of opposition to England was agitated. In this controversy, it became early enlisted, and uniformly on the popular side; and was distinguished for its ardent, decided, and independent patriotism, and for its intelligence and originality."

Meanwhile, except for choosing a representative to the General Court and providing the required list of jurors, the business of the town meetings was purely local: building and maintenance of roads and bridges and schools; support for widows and the poor; a steeple for the meetinghouse, a fence around the burying place, payments to the minister and a pall for funerals to be provided at the town's expense. As soon as the steeple was finished, one of the leading citizens donated a bell. In his simple but eloquent letter of gift, we sense his feeling for the community: "Whereas by the all disposing Providence of God by whom the bounds of men's habitations are set, I have had my residence within the bounds of the Town of Lincoln — wherein I have lived in unity and good agreement, and for the love and regard that I have to the inhabitants of said Town, I do hereby give to the inhabitants of said town the Bell that now hangs upon the Steeple — for the Town's use forever. Hereunto I subscribe your hearty Friend and humble Servant, Joseph Brooks."

Two decades later, his bell would rouse the Lincoln minutemen in the early hours of an April morning. But for the time being things were peaceful. The only hint of foreign strife during Lincoln's first years is an article in the warrant for the town meeting of September 1754: "To know the Towns mind respecting the part of the Excise Bill which relates to the private consumption of Wines and Spirits Distilled." This tax, which was to be approved later in the month by the Concord town meeting "after a considerable debate thereon," had for its principal purpose the financing of the war against the French in Canada. Though Lincoln as well as its mother town may have taken some small part in the French and Indian War (as it later came to be called), it was the events immediately following the war that were to lead to the eventual break with England. One of these was passage by Parliament of the Sugar Act in 1764. From the early account books that have come down to us, two facts are clear. First, that our forebears liked their rum and their molasses; in Lincoln in 1760, both sold briskly at 4 shillings a quart. Second, that hard currency was scarce. By enforcing duties on trade with the foreign West Indies, by forbidding the importation of rum and spirits from the islands, the Sugar Act would at once reduce the supply of hard liquor and hard money — an intolerable combination. A year later the Stamp Act led to the first outburst of violence — riots in Boston and the burning of Lieutenant Governor Hutchinson's house. But the first official recognition by Lincoln of the growing crisis followed the passage of the Townshend Acts imposing import duties on glass, lead, painters' colors, paper, and tea — the revenue from which was to be used to pay fixed salaries to the colonial governors and other royal officials. (It is interesting to speculate whether, had this tax existed in 1754 and Governor Shirley been independent of the General Court for his salary, he would ever have allowed Lincoln to be born.) Boston's response to the Townshend Acts was to adopt a non-importation agreement, which was then circulated to other towns for their endorsement. On January 4, 1768, the following article came before the Lincoln town meeting: "To see if the Town will concur with the Town of Boston in their town Meeting of the 28th of October last with regard to incourage the produce and manufactures of this province and to lessen the use of Superfluites imported from abroad." More conservative than their Boston brethren, the citizens of Lincoln twice deferred action; finally on March 5, 1770 (the very day of the Boston Massacre), they voted "that they will not Purchase any one article of any

Person that imports goods contrary to the agreement of the marchants in the Town of Boston."

Tension continued to mount throughout the Colony. Late in 1772 Boston's Samuel Adams — cousin of John, at the age of fifty a failure in business but a leader in politics — took the lead in forming eighty town Committees of Correspondence and drafting a declaration of colonial rights to be submitted to each town for local approval. Acting with due deliberation, the citizens of Lincoln on January 25, 1773, appointed a committee to consider the matter and report back within a fortnight. Their report was unequivocal: ". . . We hereby assure that we will not be wanting in our assistance according to our ability, in the prosecuting all lawful and constitutional measures as shall be thought proper for the continuance of all our rights, privileges and liberties, both civil and religious, being of opinion that a steady united persevering conduct in a constitutional way is the best means under God for obtaining the redress of all our grievances." Not till early November, however, did Lincoln appoint its own Committee of Correspondence, consisting of Deacon Samuel Farrar, Captain Eleazer Brooks and Captain Abijah Peirce.

Six weeks later, again under Sam Adams' leadership, a mob of citizens crudely got up as Indians dumped three shiploads of tea into Boston Harbor, in symbolic protest

against taxation from abroad. This incident, which infuri-
ated the British Parliament and led to the closing of the
Port of Boston, elicited from the little town of Lincoln one
of the most eloquent statements of the conscientious colonist's position. At a special town meeting on December 27,
1773, the voters endorsed a letter to the Boston Committee
of Correspondence that reflects the inner conflict between
loyalty to the mother country on the one hand, and commitment to fight for human rights on the other. The letter,
quoted here in part, is believed to have been composed by
Captain Eleazer Brooks, who was soon to resign his commission in the British militia, take part as a private citizen
in the battle at Concord Bridge, and rise to the rank of
Brigadier General in the Revolutionary Militia.

"Gentlemen, — We have read your letter, enclosing the
proceedings of the town of Boston at their late meeting . . .
in which . . . you desire our advice and to be acquainted
with the sense of this town respecting the present gloomy
situation of our public affairs. We rejoice at every appearance of public virtue, and resolution in the cause of liberty;
inasmuch as, upon our own virtue and resolution, under
Divine Providence, depends the preservation of all our
rights and privileges.

"We apprehend, that we, in America, have rights, privileges, and property, of our own, as well as the rest of man-
kind; and that we have the right of self-preservation, as
well as all other beings. And we are constrained to say,
that after the most careful and mature deliberation, according to our capacities, weighing the arguments on both sides,
we apprehend our rights and privileges have been infringed
in many glaring instances, which we mean not to enumer-
ate, among which the late ministerial plan, mentioned in
your letter, is not the least . . .

"The situation of our public affairs growing more alarming, and having heretofore tried the force of petitions and

remonstrances and finding no redress; we, the inhabitants of this town, have now come into a full determination and settled resolution, not to purchase, nor to use any tea, nor suffer it to be purchased or used in our families, so long as there is any duty laid on such tea by an act of the British Parliament. And we will hold and esteem such, as do use such tea, enemies to their country; and we will treat them with the greatest neglect. And we beg leave to recommend it to the several towns within this province, who have not done it, to go and do likewise . . .

"We trust we have courage and resolution sufficient to encounter all the horrors of war in the defence of those rights and privileges, civil and religious, which we esteem more valuable than our lives. And we do hereby assure, not only the town of Boston, but the world, that whenever we shall have a clear call from Heaven, we are ready to join with our brethren to face the formidable forces, rather than tamely to surrender up our rights and privileges into the hands of any of our own species, not distinguished from ourselves, except to be in disposition to enslave us. At the same time, we have the highest esteem for all lawful authority; and rejoice in our connexion with Great Britain, so long as we can enjoy our charter rights and privileges."

Preserved in the Eleazer Brooks papers are two documents — one signed by 52 residents of Lincoln, the other by 82 — incorporating the essence of this letter. As it approached its twentieth birthday, Lincoln, along with the neighboring towns, was committed (but only as a last resort) to the irreversible act of war.

Up till now, there had been no "clear call from Heaven." As that fiery patriot Dr. Joseph Warren (soon to be killed at Bunker Hill) wrote to a friend, probably not fifty men in the colony expected that it would actually come to a fight. But on the eve of a major conflict events often seem to take on their own momentum, until at some indefinable moment they pass the point of no return. If one had to pick such a moment on the road to our Revolution, it would be the arrival in Boston on May 10, 1774, of His Majesty's ship *Lively*, with a new set of orders from London. The British Parliament, whose Tory leadership had little respect for the fighting ability of the American "peasants" if it should come to a showdown, had imposed a number of punitive measures in addition to the Boston Port Bill. These included a law "for the better regulating the government of the Massachusetts Bay," which took back from the colonists the right to choose their own officials and even went so far as to forbid town meetings except for the purpose of electing town officers — a regulation, however, that was generally ignored.

Governor Hutchinson, who had devoted so much of his life to the welfare of the Bay Colony and had written her history, departed for England to report to his superiors, unaware that he was never to return. His successor, General Gage, appeared in Boston with four regiments under his command. More were brought in during the summer, until there were some five thousand troops billeted in the beleaguered town. With normal business at a standstill, the plight of the civilian population was becoming acute. Nearby Massachusetts towns and the more distant colonies came to the rescue with supplies brought in by land over the Neck, and with funds for the unemployed and poverty-stricken. In the warrant for the Lincoln town meeting of January 5, 1775, we find an article: "To know whether the town will contribute any thing for the relief of the poor people in Boston and Charlestown." The vote was affirmative and a committee was chosen "to draught a subscription for said purpose."

With the lid clamped down, the political pot boiled more dangerously than ever. In defiance of the Governor, a Provincial Congress had been called to meet in Concord on

October 11, 1774. Delegates were chosen in the same manner as those to the General Court, which had been virtually
suspended. Thinking to forestall and defuse this illegal assembly, Gage quickly summoned a meeting of the General
Court at Salem. (With the Port of Boston closed, Salem was
the temporary capital.) At a special Lincoln town meeting
on September 29 "the Selectmen put the question to the
town whether they would chuse a Representative to represent them at the Great and General Court to be convened
held and kept at Salem on Wednesday ye 5th day of October
next." The vote was affirmative and Eleazer Brooks was
chosen. This was the historic meeting which General Gage
attempted to cancel at the last minute when he realized
how strong had become the spirit of revolt. The towns went
ahead and sent delegates despite the executive prohibitions,
anticipating that the official meeting would be dissolved by
the governor, but instructing their representatives to "ad-
here firmly to the Charter of this Province" and to arrange
to meet later with members from the other towns in a Provincial Congress. So it happened. "With cautious courtesy
they [the ninety delegates] awaited . . . the attendance of
the governor, or other constitutional officer, to administer
the usual oaths. When it became certain . . . that the presence of the chief magistrate could no longer be expected, a
convention was organized . . ." The Court voted to "resolve
itself into a Provincial Congress, to be joined by other persons as have been or shall be chosen for such purpose," and
to adjourn to the Court House at Concord. Secret sessions
were held there and later in Lexington. Before adjourn-
ment, a public letter was sent to General Gage protesting
his hostile preparations which threatened "To involve us in
all the confusion and horrors of a civil war." The Congress
continued to meet at intervals.

Meanwhile, the other colonies, sympathetic with Boston's
plight and aware of the threat to them all, had sent dele-

gates to Philadelphia to the First Continental Congress, which declared the "intolerable acts" imposed on Massachusetts — represented by Samuel and John Adams — as "unpolitic, unjust, cruel and unconstitutional." With publication of this Declaration of Rights and Grievances, war had come one step closer.

Lincoln's first official act anticipating possible hostilities took place at the same January town meeting that voted to help the poor people of Boston, and that had established a Committee of Inspection at the behest of the Continental Congress. "On the third article, voted to make some allowance to minute men if they should be drawn out — voted the further consideration of this article be referred to next March meeting." The Provincial Congress had, some ten weeks earlier, established a committee of safety which was to purchase arms and reorganize the militia. A special force was recruited to "equip and hold itself in readiness, at the shortest notice from the committee of safety, to march to the place of rendezvous."

On February 23, 1775, the committee sent instructions to the towns for assembling the militia and the minutemen. To Concord they dispatched not only military stores but also, in the best tradition of New England, twenty hogsheads of molasses and the same of rum. The beverage that blessed her barn-raisings and built her stone walls would be ready to fortify her defenders.

Lincoln's response to the summons from the committee must have been reasonably prompt, since by March 6 the town was concerned with "paying ye minute men for their discipline" (i.e., their military training). The matter was twice deferred, but on March 20 it was voted "that the sum of fifty two pounds four shillings be and is hereby granted to provide for those persons who have inlisted as minite men each one a bayonet belt catridge box steal ramer gun stock and knapsack: they to attend military exercise four hours in a day twice in a week till the first day of May next . . ." They were to have less than a month of exercise before facing the real thing.

In early April, attending a session of the Provincial Congress in Concord, James Warren wrote to his wife, Mercy: "Last week things wore a rather favorable aspect, but alas how uncertain are our prospects . . . We are no longer at a loss what is Intended us by our dear Mother. We have ask'd for Bread and she gives us a Stone, and a serpent for a Fish . . . All things wear a warlike appearance here. This Town is full of Cannon, ammunition, stores, etc. and the [British] Army long for them and they want nothing but strength to Induce an attempt on them. The people are ready and determine to defend this country Inch by Inch."

Spies kept the British well informed of these preparations for war. Disguised as a patriot, a gunsmith named John Howe was welcomed by the rebel leaders in Concord and shown all their secret stores. On his way back to Boston, he stopped at a small house in Lincoln. "I found it inhabited by an old man and his wife; the old man was cleaning his gun. I asked him what he was going to kill, as he was so old, I should not think he could take sight at any game; he said there was a flock of red coats at Boston, which he expected would be here soon; he meant to try and hit some of them, as he expected they would be very good marks. I asked him when they were expected out; he replied he should not think strange if they should come before morning . . . I asked him how old he was; he said seventy-seven, and never was killed yet."

*   *   *

When the word came, it came in the night. For Lincoln, more specifically, it came some time after one o'clock in the morning of April 19, on a lonely stretch of the road between Lexington and Concord.

"Listen my children and you shall hear/ Of the midnight ride of Paul Revere." What the children heard — and have been hearing for generations — was stirring verse but shaky history. As most of us are now aware, Longfellow, writing in 1863, had the general idea but was confused about the details. The confusion begins with the hanging of the lanterns in the belfry of Boston's Old North Church: "One if by land, and two, if by sea,/ And I on the opposite shore will be." The "sea," though convenient for the rhyme, was actually the placid waters of the lower Charles River. Revere was not waiting booted and spurred on the opposite shore; he was supervising the hanging of the lanterns, which were a signal, not *to* him but *from* him, in case he was unable to elude the British fleet and cross the river to spread the alarm. And of course he never got to "the bridge in Concord town," but was captured by a British patrol in North Lincoln.

The picture of a solitary horseman galloping through the night into history has been long since discredited. Indeed the pendulum has swung so far the other way that Esther Forbes, when she was writing her classic biography of Paul Revere, was asked by several super-sceptics whether he ever rode at all! The fact is that he was the most experienced courier in the patriots' cause, chosen for this crucial and dangerous mission because of his cleverness and courage. Though he failed to get all the way to Concord, he did accomplish his main purpose, stated in his instructions from Joseph Warren: "to go to Lexington, and inform Mr. Samuel Adams, and the Hon. John Hancock, Esq., that there was a number of Soldiers [about 700 men] ... marching to the bottom of the Common, where was a number of boats to receive them; it was supposed that they were going to Lexington ... to take *them* [i.e., Adams and Hancock], or to go to Concord, to distroy the Colony Stores."

The events of that night and the following day have been

written about to a fare-thee-well. Every scrap of evidence
has been weighed, every contemporary account has been
squeezed dry. These accounts are occasionally conflicting
and tantalizingly brief. In contrast to later commanders,
from Ulysses S. Grant to Dwight D. Eisenhower, the leaders
of the embattled farmers, though aware that they were
making history, were not concerned with writing their
memoirs. Modern historians, like paleontologists reconstructing a fossil skeleton, have had to fit the pieces together
as best they could. Some major and many minor bones are
missing, but the result of their labors shows what diligent
digging and fine sifting can accomplish.

*   *   *

The little drama, so far as it concerns Lincoln, falls naturally into three acts. ACT ONE, of short duration, and involving a fairly small cast (though Revere is never alone on
the stage), is pleasantly romantic. SCENE: The Lexington-
Concord road. TIME: Between one and two in the morning. The apple trees are white in the moonlight, for spring
has come a month early. The previous evening a patrol of
British officers from Boston had passed through Lexington,
and three minutemen had volunteered to ride after them
and learn what they were up to. Unhappily these scouts
had come unawares upon the officers near Lincoln's Folly
Pond, been forced at gunpoint to dismount, and were now
being held captive in an adjacent pasture.

In Lexington, while the minutemen were assembling in
the village green, Paul Revere had joined the courier who
came by land, Major William Dawes. After reporting to
Adams and Hancock, the two of them set out on the road
to Concord. Soon they were overtaken and joined by a
young Concordian and "high Son of Liberty," Dr. Samuel
Prescott, who had been courting his girl in Lexington.

As the curtain rises, they are approaching the Lincoln

line. Prescott, accompanied by Dawes, falls behind to rouse a household along the road. Here he finds his friend Nathaniel Baker, a Lincoln minuteman, also out courting his girl. Baker rides off to give the alarm in South Lincoln. Prescott and Dawes hurry on after Revere. Suddenly two mounted officers appear from beneath a tree into the moonlight. Revere thinks to capture them, or at least to push through. But another pair emerges from the pasture where the three Lexington scouts are already held captive. Now Revere, turning off the road, runs smack into the six British soldiers who were guarding the prisoners; they seize his bridle and force him to dismount. Dawes turns and gallops back up the road, the enemy at his heels. Racing to the nearest farmhouse, he shouts: "Halloo, my boys! I've got two of 'em." He stops so abruptly that he falls off his horse. But he has outwitted his pursuers. Fearing an ambush, they ride away. (The house was empty.)

Revere and his captors ride back toward Lexington. The noise of their passing wakes Josiah Nelson, Lincoln minuteman charged with the duty of warning Bedford should the British march on Concord. His wife, mistaking the horsemen for farmers on the way to market, sends her husband out to get the latest news. Nelson leaps from bed, slips on his breeches and hurries to the door without shoes or hat. Running in among the horsemen, not looking up to see who they are, he cries out: "Have you heard anything about when the Regulars are coming out?" One of the officers draws his sword, and crying, "We will let you know when they are coming!" strikes him on the crown of his head, cutting a long gash. Blood trickles over his face and drips to the ground — the first blood shed in the Revolution. Released, but on threat of death if he leaves his house, Nelson waits till the British are out of sight, then saddles his mare and rides to Bedford, giving the alarm.

What of Prescott? A good horseman, and knowing the

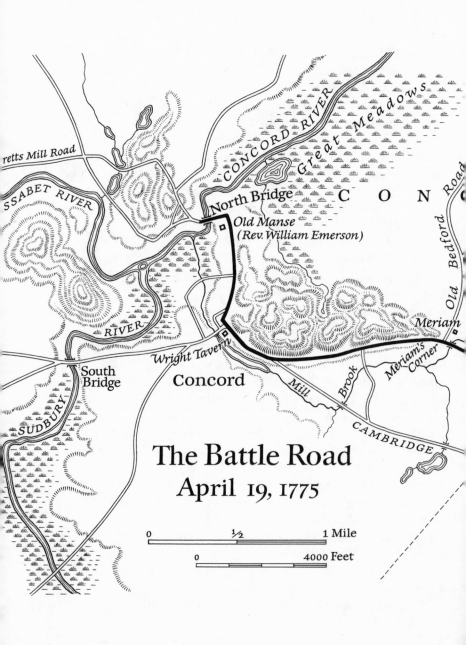

retts Mill Road

ASSABET RIVER

CONCORD RIVER

Great Meadows

North Bridge

CON

Old Manse
(Rev. William Emerson)

RIVER

Old Bedford Road

Meriam

Wright Tavern

Meriam's Corner

South Bridge

Concord

Mill

Brook

SUDBURY

CAMBRIDGE

The Battle Road
April 19, 1775

0   ½   1 Mile

0   4000 Feet

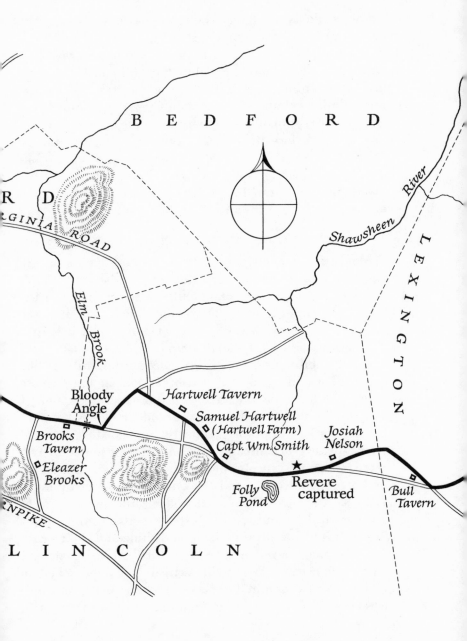

BEDFORD

Shawsheen River

LEXINGTON

VIRGINIA ROAD

Elm Brook

Bloody
Angle

Hartwell Tavern

Samuel Hartwell
(Hartwell Farm)

Capt. Wm. Smith

Josiah
Nelson

Brooks
Tavern

Eleazer
Brooks

★ Revere
captured

Folly
Pond

Bull
Tavern

TURNPIKE

LINCOLN

terrain as the others do not, he jumps a stone wall and circles toward Concord, stopping at the farm of Sergeant Samuel Hartwell, who prepares to join his company while his
wife Mary walks alone through the night to wake their
neighbor William Smith, Captain of the Lincoln minutemen. Smith gallops off to Lincoln Center to assemble the
two Lincoln companies and march them to Concord, where
they arrive before those of any other neighboring towns.
So while Prescott is completing Revere's mission in Concord, the bell hung two decades ago in the steeple of the
meetinghouse, gift of Joseph Brooks to the new-born town
of Lincoln, shatters the silence of the night.

ACT TWO. Later the same morning.

Mary Hartwell, whose husband rode off hours ago to
join the Lincoln minutemen, has finished the farm chores
and is attending to her young children when she hears the
tramp of marching men. Down the Bay Road comes the
bright red line of British grenadiers and light infantry.
"The army of the King marched up in fine order," she later
recalled, "and their bayonets glistened in the sunlight like
a field of waving grain. If it hadn't been for the purpose
they came for, I should say it was the handsomest sight I
ever saw in my life." Twenty-year-old Thaddeus Blood of
the Concord militia was similarly impressed. "About 4
oclock the several companies of Concord were joined by two
companies from Lincoln, the militia company commanded
by Colonel Pierce . . . and the minute company by Capt.
Wm. Smith. . . . We . . . marched in order to the end of
Meriams hill . . . and saw the British troops a coming down
Brooks hill. The sun was rising and shined on their arms,
and they made a noble appearance in their red coats and
glistening arms." When the British had approached to
within about a hundred rods, recalled Amos Barrett, "we
was ordered to the about face and march before them with

our Droms and fifes agoing and also the B[ritish] we had
grand musick." After a brief halt at the liberty pole in the
center of town (which the British subsequently chopped
down) the provincials retreated through the burying
ground and on to the North Bridge, crossed over, and took
their stand on the hill beyond, where they were joined by
the companies from Lincoln, Acton, and Bedford, and
groups from other nearby towns, eventually making a force
of over 400 men.

"The shot heard round the world" has been in orbit now
for two hundred years. The circumstances of its firing are
in all the schoolbooks. It is interesting that Eleazer Brooks
should be one of those who insisted that the first shot must
not be ours. "Let us go and meet them," said one of the
company on the hillside, as the redcoats crossed the river
and formed ranks by the bridge. "No," he replied, "it will
not do for *us* to begin the war." Colonel Barrett of the Concord militia, who was in command, took the same position.
Writes Thaddeus Blood: "I heard him several times charge
the companies not to fire first, as we were marching to the
bridge." The killing, of course, had already begun in Lexington, but this was not yet known for sure. What trig-
gered the fighting was "an unusual smoke" rising from the
center of Concord, where the Regulars were destroying any
stores they could find. "Will you let them burn the town
down?" cried adjutant Joseph Hosmer. The provincials
decided to attack. Captain Smith of Lincoln offered his
company to dislodge the British from the bridge. But
Major Buttrick and Captain Davis of Acton decided that
Davis' men should be put in front, since only they had
bayonets.

Deliberately, to the tune of "The White Cockade" played
by fife and drum, the provincials marched down the hill
and on to the road to the bridge, hastening their pace when
the redcoats, having recrossed to the town side, began to

tear up the planks. Two or three warning shots from the British splashed into the water, then a single aimed shot, then a volley. "Their balls whistled well," wrote Amos Barrett later. Two provincials dropped dead. "Fire, fellow soldiers," cried Major Buttrick, "for God's sake, fire!" A volley of bullets poured into the British ranks. As they turned and fled back toward the town, they left two of their number behind, to be buried where they fell.

"Now the war has begun," said Noah Parkhurst of Lincoln to his friend Amos Baker, "and no one knows when it will end."

ACT THREE. The Concord-Lexington road. Early afternoon.

The Americans did not immediately follow up their advantage. Probably they could not have done so. They were civilians in arms, not trained troops; in a conventional face-to-face battle with the Regulars, they might have come out second-best. Their main object was to get the British out of Concord, and the longer they waited, the more their numbers were swelled by militia from the more distant towns.

The British were resting, and caring for their wounded. The Reverend William Emerson — Concord's warlike minister who had spurred on the provincials and watched the battle from the grounds of the Old Manse — was puzzled by the redcoats' apparent indecisiveness: "Y^e enemy by y^r Marches and counter Marches discor^d gt [great] Feekelness and Inconstancy of Mind, sometimes advancing sometimes returning to y^r former Posts, till at Length they quitted ye Town, and retreated by ye Wayy [they] came." The retreat to Charlestown began about noon. Now the "detached parties of Bushmen," as General Gage had termed the provincials, were to get their chance.

The country around Concord is "an immensely strong one" for defense, reported the British spies who had scouted

it a few weeks earlier. Certainly at that time it was well
suited for what we now call guerrilla warfare, which can
be extraordinarily effective against the best-organized military might. And the redcoats at Concord were not well-
organized to deal with such an ungentlemanly form of
combat. Moreover they were not dealing with acquiescent
English peasants but with freeholders whose homes and
fields and orchards had been won by their ancestors' toil —
a class of independent farmers that was disappearing from
the old country, where, in the words of a contemporary
writer, they had been "the most useful sets of men that
could be found in this or any kingdom."

Over seventy-five Lincoln men are known to have been
under arms on April 19. Among those at the bridge was
Amos Baker, who had been roused the night before by his
brother Nathaniel. Three quarters of a century later, at the
age of ninety-four, he recalled the Concord fight. His father, his four brothers, and his brother-in-law were all at
his side. "After the fight at the bridge, I saw nothing more

of them, and did not know whether they were alive or dead, until I found two of my brothers engaged in the pursuit near Lexington meeting-house." Nathaniel followed the enemy to Charlestown. He recalls the informality of the minutemen's arms: "I believe I was the only man from Lincoln that had a bayonet. My father got it in the time of the French war . . . Abijah Pierce of Lincoln, the colonel of the minutemen, went up armed with nothing but a cane." When the skirmish was over, he "got the gun of one of the British soldiers who was killed at the bridge."

There are few contemporary accounts of the retreat through North Lincoln to Lexington, but they are sufficient to re-create the scene. The dirt road is rough and winding, following the contours of the land. At Meriam's Corner, less than a mile west of the Concord-Lincoln line, the long ridge to the north of the road (the same that sheltered the early settlers from the winter wind) peters out; the flat meadows (which sustained their crops and cattle) begin. Just beyond the joining with the old Bedford road, a narrow bridge crosses a branch of Mill Brook. The British are marching "with very slow, but steady step, without music, or a word spoken that could be heard." The provincials from the Concord fight, now reinforced by men from Sudbury, hasten across the Great Meadows; minutemen from Billerica and Chelmsford, Reading and Woburn, hurry down the Bedford road, others from East Sudbury and Framingham arrive from the south. The redcoats are crowded together as they cross the little bride over Mill Brook. Suddenly there is a crash of musketry, "A grait many Lay dead," recalls Amos Barrett, "and the Road was bloddy." The running fight has begun.

General Gage predicted correctly how the "Bushmen" would behave. "Should hostilities unhappily commence, the first opposition would be irregular impetuous and incessant from the numerous Bodys that would swarm to the place of action, and all actuated by an enthusiasm wild and ungovernable . . . A regular encampment seems abhorrent to the genius and inclination of the People, much more is to be apprehended from their patience and cunning, in forming ambushments."

Now as the tired redcoats, sweltering in their heavy woolen uniforms, plod doggedly through the warm April afternoon, the Americans' "ambushments" take deadly effect. Just inside the Lincoln line the old road, bordered by stone walls and slightly sunken below the level of the surrounding terrain, turns sharply north up a gentle slope; to the west stands a grove of great trees, to the east high bushes backed by a swamp. Each man on his own, the minutemen run ahead through the woods and fields and orchards, and take cover behind tree trunks and walls. As the redcoats get within range (close range, for these are smoothbore muskets, not rifles), they are met by a hail of lead from an unseen enemy. Eight fall dead or dying, along the short stretch of road ever since known as the "Bloody Angle." Nor do the inexperienced provincials go scot-free; failing to detect the light infantry protecting the British flanks, some are surprised and shot in the back. But their "wild and ungovernable" enthusiasm never falters, and they keep the upper hand.

During that short march through Lincoln, the British, brave as they were, became at last disorganized. An ensign has recorded their mounting panic: "All the hills on each side of us were covered with rebels . . . so that they kept the road always lined and a very hot fire on us without intermission; we at first kept our order and returned their fire as hot as we received it, but when we arrived within a mile of Lexington, our ammunition began to fail, and the light companies were so fatigued with flanking they were scarce able to act, and a great number of wounded scarce able to get forward, made a great confusion . . ." As they passed

the Hartwell farm, the redcoats (Mary Hartwell later recalled) were wild with rage. "I heard musket shots just below the old Brooks Tavern, and trembled, believing that
our folks were killed. Some of the rough, angry redcoats
rushed up to this house and fired in, but fortunately for me
and the children the shots went into the garret and we were
safe." In Lexington the British finally met the relief expedition under Lord Percy; in Percy's own words, it saved
them from "inevitable destruction," though some of the
bitterest fighting of the day was still to take place before
the pursuit finally ended at dusk in Charlestown. "The in-
surrection here," reported Percy next day, "[will not] turn
out so despicable as it is perhaps imagined at home. For my
part, I never believed, I confess, that they would have attacked the King's troops, or have had the perseverance I
found in them yesterday."

EPILOGUE. Lincoln. The following morning.

Mary Hartwell had not been able to sleep that night,
thinking of the British soldiers lying dead by the roadside.
Setting out next morning with her children for the home of
her father, Ephraim Flint, she saw before her on the narrow road two elderly neighbors with a yoke of oxen and a
cart in which lay the bodies, clad in their fine red uniforms,
of five British grenadiers. As the rude hearse creaked
slowly on, she followed it reverently — the first mourner
(as she used afterward to say), the only mourner, of the
fallen enemy. When the old men reached Lincoln Center,
they turned down past the Flint homestead to the burying
ground which lay in the field beyond. There, on a little
knoll apart from where the founders of the town were sleeping, they spaded out a square grave, and into this they low-
ered the five soldiers of King George. As she watched,
Mary Hartwell forgot her ill feelings toward them of the
day before. She recalled "thinking of the wives, parents

and children away across the ocean who could never see their loved ones again."

And so the fallen soldiers lay forgotten, while generations were born and died, and white oaks grew up to shade the little knoll. More than a century after the battle, the citizens of Lincoln erected a simple monument where they were thought to rest. When at length their bones were accidentally unearthed nearby, they were no longer lying apart from their fellows.

CHAPTER 8 ⌝

"We are not to expect to be translated from despotism to liberty in a featherbed."
— Thomas Jefferson to the Marquis de Lafayette

The Price of War

A month after the battle, John Adams wrote from Philadelphia to James Warren: "The Martial Spirit throughout this Province is astonishing, it arose all of a sudden, since the News of the Battle of Lexington." By contrast, Lincoln's Amos Baker concludes his account of the stirring events of April 19, 1775, with the laconic remark: "I verily believe that I felt better that day, take it all the day through, than if I had staid at home." This choice bit of New England understatement was made many years after the event, yet it probably reflects fairly accurately the matter-of-fact attitude that soon prevailed toward the life-and-death struggle that had begun so dramatically on the banks of the Concord River. Though for the next six years the American colonies would encounter, in Eleazer Brooks's phrase, all the horrors of war, the blood would be shed elsewhere. Lincoln farmers were embattled only when their families and farms were immediately threatened; once the excitement of the first encounter had subsided, there was no rush of volunteers to serve under General Washington in the newly formed Continental Army. No universal draft compelled military service. The historian Charles Francis Adams, who himself served through four years of the Civil

War, notes with some scorn that in both our major conflicts the Massachusetts towns, Lincoln included, displayed a lack of the "military instinct," the first burst of zeal being followed by "coolness and huckstering. Patriotism was bought and sold."

Certainly Lincoln kept cool. Here as elsewhere, the town records of the period do sometimes resemble a commercial payroll, with long lists of bounties paid for military service in Boston, Cambridge, Roxbury, and Dorchester; in Saratoga and Ticonderoga and Canada: "On the second article voted that six pounds six shillings and eightpence be granted to those non commission officers and solgers that shall inlist themselves into the present expedition to Canady." These men were procured by the town officials to meet the quota imposed on each town by the General Court. In the summer of 1778, the town voted to assume "all future expenses of carrying on the present war so far as respects procuring of men when called for by lawful authority." A committee was then appointed "for hiring men for the present campaign."

The costs involved were enormous. Eighteen months later it was voted "that the sum of fifteen thousand eight hundred and forty pounds be granted for the purpose of paying eleven three months men now in the Militia Department." Even more expensive than buying men was buying meat. In January 1781, over sixteeen thousand pounds was appropriated to procure beef for the army. Such figures obviously reflect rampant inflation of the currency. When, on orders from the General Court, the town was "classed for the purpose of procuring men for services in the War," each class being obliged to procure one man, a committee was appointed to determine the value in hard money that each class spent and spread it evenly over the whole town.

Mr. Adams calls it huckstering. But with no strong central government to guarantee a soldier's pay, one could hardly expect the New England farmer to enlist willingly for a three-year stint with the regular army while his acres deteriorated and his family starved. Such master rolls as have survived indicate that Lincoln men were not slow to join the armed forces. Sixty-two minutemen, for example, fought under the command of Captain William Smith on the nineteenth of April and about a hundred all together served for longer or shorter periods at other times in the war. This was out of a total of 187 male inhabitants over the age of sixteen.

To be sure, the militia system was inadequate for carrying on a continental war. Men hired for a period of a few months would go home when their tour of duty was up, sometimes on the eve of a battle. It was Washington's Continental Army, with its long enlistments, that bore the brunt of the fighting. Lincoln contributed a number of volunteers. As early as March 1776, the town was voting to relieve from the highway rate "those persons listed in the Continental Army." And once the fighting had begun, the town was apparently united in its loyalties. Unlike Concord, whose jail bulged with political as well as military prisoners, Lincoln had no problem with Tories; a community of farmers, it contained few if any rich merchants or professional men with a personal stake in the status quo. Nevertheless, in obedience to an act of the General Court, the town meeting dutifully agreed to bring to trial any persons that were found to be "inimically disposed" toward the patriots' cause. But the fact is that the most prominent citizen who could be expected to take the British side — the town's founding father, Chambers Russell — had returned in 1766 to England, where he died shortly after his arrival. His nephew, Dr. Charles Russell, who inherited his uncle's Lincoln property, had been pronounced a Tory and his estate confiscated. He had taken a ship for Antigua, where his family had an estate. In so doing he had left a big hole in the tax rolls.

The people of Lincoln, like their compatriots elsewhere, were faced with a real threat which had nothing to do with any lingering friendliness toward Great Britain. This was the threat of shortages, high prices, and inflation. Though Lincoln, along with its neighbors, had prudently declined to lend money on interest to the State Treasury, the town obeyed the requirement of the General Court that it provide clothing as well as food to the army. Sample prices give an idea of what was happening. In 1778 a "pair of good shoes" already cost 2 pounds 16 shillings; in 1780 it was 3 pounds 16 shillings. The account books of the Lincoln tradesman Joshua Child show a gallon of rum selling at 16 shillings in 1766. In 1779, the official price was set at 4 pounds 16 shillings. Such prices are staggering when compared, for example, with the 3 shillings per day that the town paid for work on the roads. By the summer of 1779 the situation had become so acute that representatives from 121 Massachusetts towns met in Concord to set up a system of price controls on imported and domestic products, journeymen's wages, and innkeepers' charges. Formerly approved by the Lincoln town meeting, they give a hair-raising picture of the high cost of living in wartime New England.

The first category on the list, "West Indies goods Imported," shows what the war had done to our trade with the islands. Besides the leap in price of rum, we find coffee selling at 18 shillings and chocolate at 24 shillings a pound. "Bohea Tea" was 5 pounds 16 shillings a pound; salt 10 pounds 10 shillings per bushel.

"Country Produce" was more reasonable but still high: Beef at 5 shillings, salt pork at 12 shillings, and butter at 11 shillings per pound. Cider, the staple drink of the Colonial farmer, was now 5 pounds a barrel. The ceiling on men's shoes was 6 pounds a pair — the same as that for "a new ax." A "good common saddle" sold for 40 pounds; the best saddles for 60.

Carpenters and masons could both charge 60 shillings a day, but the most a housemaid might demand was 30 shillings a week. Innkeepers were allowed to charge 15 shillings for a "Mug of West India Phlip"; 12 shillings if made with New England rum. A "common dinner" was 12 shillings, a "good dinner" 20.

Though it looked well on paper, this elaborate attempt at price-fixing failed in practice and was eventually scrapped. Enforcement collapsed, as towns began to accuse each other of breaking the compact. Shortages of both goods and labor kept prices soaring. Paper money issued by the Continental Congress dropped in value to the point where the government decided to redeem it at the rate of one "new Tenure" to forty old. Even that failed; it kept on slipping till it was of virtually no value — "not worth a continental." Meanwhile there were more soldiers' bounties to pay off and heavier taxes from the state (which the province had now become), over which the town had no control. There is a note of near panic in the town meeting vote of July 23, 1782, "that they will exert themselves to procure money for the last State Tax and to pay it between this time and the next Saturday at 4 o'clock P.M."

One continuing local obligation was the minister's salary. During the final years of the war it appears to have more than quadrupled. When Charles Stearns succeeded William Lawrence in 1781, the town agreed to pay him in "hard money," defined later as "gold or silver or other money equivalent." He was fortunate. Three years later, the value in specie of the old currency held in the town treasury had dropped to approximately 1 to 78.

The financial crisis was due in part to the governmental chaos that succeeded the break with Britain. Less than two months after the first shots had been fired at Lexington and

Concord, the Provincial Congress had sought help and direction from the Continental Congress in Philadelphia: "The embarrassments, delays, disappointments, and obstructions for the preservation of our lives, and . . . property, are so great — they cannot be enumerated; and that is chiefly to be attributed to our want of a settled civil polity." The Congress finally recommended that each sovereign state in the Federation draw up its own constitution. Initially the task was undertaken by the Massachusetts House of Representatives. But the resulting document, though approved by a State Convention, instantly ran into trouble when it was submitted to the towns for approval in the spring of 1778. Concord had claimed from the beginning that the House of Representatives was not the proper body to form a Constitution: "The inhabitants at large, not the assembly, should attend to this business." On May 8, Lincoln's town meeting voted, 38 to 1, to disapprove. A year later the question came up again: "Voted. The town will not chuse at this time to have a new Constitution or form of government made." Five sixths of the towns in Massachusetts had voted likewise. As one town put it: "It entirely divests the good people of this state of many of the privileges that God and nature has given them." At length, following Concord's recommendation, a special Constitutional Convention was called in Cambridge, the delegates chosen by the inhabitants of the respective towns. Lincoln was represented by Eleazer Brooks. On June 5, 1780, the new draft (approved a few days earlier in Concord) came before the town. It was debated article by article. One article under "Frame of Government" was disapproved on the grounds that it did not adequately separate legislative, executive, and judicial powers. Another was rejected because the mode of representation based on "Rateable Polls in any particular corporation" — i.e., the number of qualified voters in the town — would put a small town at a great disadvantage: "So long as human nature remains the same it now is [one detects the voice of that homespun philosopher, Eleazer Brooks] each Representative will be under an undue bias in favor of the corporation he represents, therefore any large corporation having a large number of representatives will have a large and undue influence in determining any question in their own favor. Should the number of Rateable Polls in any particular corporation increase till they over balance all the others, they could completely tyrannize over all the rest, and every degree of inequality gives power for the same degree of tyranny. . . ." With these exceptions — and a provision for review within seven years — the town unanimously approved the new Constitution. Two months later John Hancock was elected the first Governor of the Commonwealth, with Lincoln giving him 42 of the 43 votes cast. For some reason, Lincoln did not start sending a representative to the state legislature until the summer of 1783. As one might expect, it was Eleazer Brooks.

The actions of the federal government appear to have been less controversial from the start. In June of 1776, the Lincoln town meeting had voted "that should the Hon^{bl} Congress for the safety of the United American Colonies declare them independent of Great Brittan, we the inhabitants of said town will solemnly engage with our lives and fortunes [to] support them in the measure." In obedience to orders from the Congress, the Declaration of Independence had been read from the pulpit and copied into the town books. When a year and a half later the Articles of Confederation were submitted to the States for ratification, Lincoln instructed its representative to "act on the Confederation and perpetual union of the United States of America as he shall think proper . . ."

But neither the adoption of the Articles of Confederation nor of states' constitutions could salvage the sinking economy. The war's end brought no relief — only a deepening of the universal depression. Trade was virtually at a standstill. Soldiers returning from the war, their farms neglected and heavily mortgaged, found the paper with which they had been paid all but worthless and in many cases were forced to resort to barter. (Isaiah Thomas of Boston, famous publisher of the *Massachusetts Spy*, advertised on November 17, 1785, that he would accept in settlements of debts due him: Indian corn, rye, wheat, wood, or flaxseed.) In Concord jail, men imprisoned for debt outnumbered all others combined.

In desperation, towns drew up lists of grievances and met in county conventions to seek means of relief. Meanwhile a rift was widening between the eastern and western parts of the state: between the maritime towns whose leaders, involved in commerce, were largely of the creditor class, and the debt-ridden farmers inland whose sole estate — their land — was in jeopardy. Boston, for example, opposed such regional meetings, deploring the fact that "there should yet remain any uneasy persons in the community, who could form the fruitless design of disturbing the tranquillity of the state by proposing the unnecessary measure of meeting by counties." The western towns, on the contrary, were on the brink of disturbing that tranquillity by resorting to force.

The people of Lincoln stood somewhere in between. In the late summer of 1786 when the situation throughout the Commonwealth had reached a state of crisis, they met "to see if the Town will choose a Committee to meet in County Convention at the house of Capt. Brown Innholder at Concord . . . to consult upon matters of Public Grievances and Embarrissments the people of this Commonwealth labor under and find out means of redress . . ." Deacon Samuel Farrar and Captain Samuel Hoar were chosen. A week later, in the western part of the state, violence at last broke

out. A band of armed men calling themselves the "regulators" stormed the Hampshire County courthouse in Northampton to prevent farms from being sold for debt, and the
court was forced to adjourn. The Worcester county courthouse, where over 3000 actions for debt were pending, was
besieged and proceedings brought to a halt. Lincoln's citizens were shocked: "Voted that this Town this day [Sep-
tember 11] declare their utter disapprobation of the disorderly proceedings of a number of persons in the Counties
of Hampshire and Worcester in the preventing the setting
of the Courts there."

The convention at Captain Brown's Tavern met early on
the morning of September Court Week. With delegates
from all over Middlesex County, it had to move to the Concord meetinghouse. Its first task was to see that the court
was allowed to sit, and to prevent violence if, as expected,
the "regulators" should appear. They did, in force, including the followers of Daniel Shays who had closed the courts
in Northampton and Worcester. Attempts to reason with
the armed mob proved fruitless. Besieged, the judges were
lucky to escape uninjured. Their mission accomplished, the
leaders departed, and a timely downpour cooled off the
would-be rioters that remained.

For the regulators it was a hollow victory; soon after, the
head of the Concord mob was captured and jailed by the
local militia. In October, the Cambridge court met without
incident. And while disorders continued throughout the
fall in the western part of the Commonwealth, they were
finally put down by the state militia — troops paid by
means of a loan from well-to-do citizens who feared an
all-out attack on their property rights. Shays's Rebellion,
in which Lincoln was never directly involved, had come to
an end.

But the issues that it had raised were real. The growing
power of the debtor classes was demonstrated in the next

gubernatorial election. In the spring of 1787 Lincoln had
to choose between the incumbent Governor James Bowdoin,
a conservative under whom the rebellion had been sup-
pressed, and John Hancock, the idol of the radicals, who
was making a return bid for office. Lincoln voted 35 for
Bowdoin, 25 for Hancock. But statewide, Hancock won. In
Massachusetts, as elsewhere in the country, the troubled
postwar years had drawn a sharp line between the men of
property and the common people — a situation of mutual
fear and distrust that could be met only by the formation
of a strong national government.

On May 14, 1787, the Convention met in Philadelphia to
frame a Federal Constitution. Laboring through the long
hot summer, delegates from the thirteen states strove to
reconcile their conflicts, driven on by dread of the conse-
quences of failure. By autumn they had achieved what
both George Washington and James Madison termed a
miracle: a signed document ready for submission to each
state for ratification. When the turn of Massachusetts came
in February, the issue still hung in the balance.

The Massachusetts convention, with 355 delegates, was
the largest of any state; finding the State House too small, it
took over the Brattle Street Church. Lincoln was again
represented by Eleazer Brooks. He witnessed a bitter debate. Here in Massachusetts — at Lexington, at Concord
Bridge, at the Bloody Angle in Lincoln — the battle for
freedom had begun. The colonists had paid the price of
war, and they were not going to give up the principles for
which they had fought. As the debate wore on, and tem-
pers frayed, the situation looked ominous. Only when the
federalists drew up a series of amendments to be recommended to the National Congress — which would lead to
the Bill of Rights — was Sam Adams willing to back the
Constitution, and bring Governor Hancock with him.
When at last the vote came, the margin — as in several

other states — was narrow: 187 ayes to 168 noes. Even federalist John Marshall admitted that only "a dread of dismemberment" led to reluctant acceptance of a strong central power. It was the price of peace.

CHAPTER 9 ⌉

"He possessed great natural endowments which he much improved
by deep research and diligent application. He was intrusted
with many important offices both military and political. In defence
of the rights of his Country he distinguished himself in Council
and in the Field."
— From the inscription on Eleazer Brooks's tombstone

Eleazer Brooks,
"The Peacemaker"

It is said that a community can be judged by the quality of its chosen leaders. Though this may not always be true in the world of professional politics, it probably holds good for the small New England village, where everyone knows his neighbor and can have his say in open town meeting. Surely there is no better way of learning what qualities are most valued, what the average citizen likes to think his town stands for, than to take a close look at the persons he elects to speak for him.

If one were to choose a single citizen whose special talents and stubborn individuality seem best to mirror Lincoln during these early years of turmoil, it would be Eleazer Brooks.* The choice is not arbitrary, since for more than three decades the townsmen themselves chose him to represent them in one capacity or another. Fortunately his papers are included among the very few contemporary Lincoln records that we have. Like those bits of scarlet uniform unearthed in the burying ground, they carry us back across two centuries. And Eleazer Brooks speaks for more than Lincoln. His long life — spanning the last half century of the Province of Massachusetts and the first three decades

* No immediate relation of the author.

of the new nation — exemplifies many of the principles on which the American experiment was founded.

In Lincoln's history, Eleazer Brooks stands in sharp contrast to the town's principal founding father, Chambers Russell. Russell was a gentleman with money and powerful connections, descendant of a prosperous merchant family, a Harvard graduate, a lawyer trained from his youth for public service. Brooks was a man of the land: a self-taught yeoman or farmer, the fifth generation on American soil.

Eleazer's great-great-grandfather, Captain Thomas Brooks (spelled Brooke), set sail from London on May 9, 1635, in the ship *Susan and Ellen*, in company with two of Concord's most distinguished first settlers, William Buttrick and the Reverend Peter Bulkeley. The following year he was granted part of the "Beaver Brook plowlands" in Watertown, but he soon moved on to Concord, where he became a captain of the militia, was elected to various town offices, and represented Concord in the General Court off and on for twenty years. Like Eleazer a century later, he was ready to fight for his rights; his name appears first on a paper addressed to the Court protesting against aggressive acts of Charles the Second. And like Eleazer, he was apparently both high-minded and shrewd, since he was appointed to carry out the laws governing the selling of liquor to the Indians (which the Puritans were not above doing to drive a hard bargain) and shortly thereafter bought the rights to the Concord fur trade from the General Court for five pounds!

Thomas' son Joshua, from whom the Lincoln Brookses are descended, was a tanner. His tannery, later described as "near to the Brooks Tavern in the Brooks Village," endured for two centuries. In what subsequently became the northwest corner of Lincoln, it was close to the spot where the retreating British, on the 19th of April, 1775, received the first volley from the farmers on their flanks, in a fight that included thirteen members of the Brooks clan.

The family prospered. It is said that they so dominated their part of town that only first names were used. In addition to the tannery they operated a brick kiln and a tavern. In 1695 Joshua the tanner and his wife, Hannah (who could not write her name, but signed with her mark), deeded to their son Daniel — Eleazer's grandfather — the land on which to build a house for his bride, Anna Meriam, a member of the neighboring family that gave its name to Meriam's Corner of Revolutionary fame. This house, which became the center of Brooks Village, was to remain in the Brooks family for 234 years, and it is still lovingly cared for by its present owner. Like so many colonial farmhouses, it started very simply and grew like a living organism, throwing out new wings as needed.

This was before the days of retirement homes, of artificial communities of senior citizens. Daniel Brooks made a place for his own parents, and he expected his children to do the same for him. When the town of Lincoln recently revised its zoning bylaw to allow apartments to be set aside in one-family houses, it had a convincing precedent in Daniel Brooks's will. Human nature being what it is, as Eleazer liked to remind us, his will left nothing to chance. If his wife outlived him, she was to have a downstairs room "with Conveniency of room in the Cellar for her use . . . Two cows to be kept for her from year to year . . . and she shall have a sufficiency of Rye and Indian Meal and a sufficiency of meat both of Beef and Pork, and Malt and Cider and Clothing of all Sorts suitable and comfortable for her, and sufficient Fire-wood . . ." While our ancestors had a well-developed sense of family obligation, they were also realistic in seeing to it that the different generations did not get in each other's way. They provided separate living quarters, often with separate stairs. At the Brooks house there were even separate wells.

Eleazer's father, Job, is identified in the Church Manual

as "a farmer in moderate circumstance." I think that he was a bit better off than that. Having inherited "the Pasture commonly called the Chestnut-Field Pasture," together with a woodlot, meadow, and upland, he increased his holdings by the purchase of no less than thirteen parcels of land between 1724 and 1738. Such was the family into which Eleazer was born on September 10, 1727. Expected to follow his father's calling, he nevertheless started early to educate himself to be more than a farmer. He read widely in mathematics, English literature, and — above all — Christian theology. He was also remembered as "a splendid athlete." At the age of thirty-five, he was "united with the Church," and shortly thereafter was appointed a Lieutenant of the British militia — the beginning of two disparate activities that he was to pursue with unremitting zeal. At thirty-six he married Mary Taylor of Concord, who died six years later.

Characterizing the Brooks family, Professor William Everett remarked that they have "a quality which can only be described by the New England word *cussedness*. You cannot make a Brooks do anything till he — or she — is quite ready to; and if the majority is against them, so much the worse for the majority. If you do succeed in absorbing a Brooks, he is leaven, salt, water, anything but dough."

Eleazer Brooks's papers are anything but doughy. Most of them are either official documents or legal and theological discussions; one could wish for something more personal. His own compositions tend to be formal and a bit long-winded, in the rhetorical style of the time. Written in a tiny hand, replete with abbreviations, they give the impression that he had much to say, and was only withheld from saying more by the high price of paper. From them, however, emerges the clear outline of a very human individual who could have sprung only from the soil of New England. Here is a voice of moderation and reason, a moralist perhaps too fond of exercising his power of logical argument. That he realized this himself is suggested by a jotting in his hand: "Lines as transcribed from an Ingenious author: Never be fond of the Formality of Disputing nor pride yourself in contradicting others upon the strength of what you have read. Let your Motive be to find out the truth, and not the Victory in Disputing. Nothing can be more disingenious [sic] or more unbecoming a well-read person, than not to yield to plain reason, and the Conviction of Clear Argument..."

In matters of religion, however, Eleazer found it hard to follow these precepts. He obviously enjoyed breaking a lance against an opponent less well armored with the Word of God. His family had always been close to the church. His uncle Joshua — a Moderator at early Precinct meetings — was a deacon, as later was Joshua's son of the same name. (Eleazer himself was chosen deacon toward the end of his life, and his son followed him.) His older brother, John, nobly upheld the family tradition when he came to choose a wife. "In 1743," recalled a descendant, "there was a great revival of religion in Concord among the young people. He visited Miss Lucy Hoar for the benefit of her pious conversation, and after making her acquaintance, offered her marriage."

Concerned though he was with the growing political crisis, Eleazer continued to be absorbed, up to the very brink of the Revolution, in fine points of church doctrine as real to him as the Stamp Act or the Boston Massacre. Looking back over his career at the time of his death, Lincoln's minister Charles Stearns notes that "In theology he was not merely conversant, but deeply versed in the science. He ... was acquainted with the different schools; knew their characteristic opinions, their modes of defending them, and their points of controversy with one another ... In the act of reasoning he was an expert." Dr. Stearns could afford to be generous, as it was not he but his predecessor, William Lawrence, who had had to field the niceties of logic which Brooks conscientiously tossed his way. Indeed, poor Mr. Lawrence must have found his learned parishioner something of a pain. There appears to have been a continuing argument when Lawrence was unlucky enough to be cornered, and between times by correspondence. "In the course of the debates that have happened between us," writes Brooks, "I think the main stress of your argument lies in pleading the late practice of the Churches." There follows a learned reference to Noah and Abraham, concluding "If so then I leave it to your Consideration, Sir, whether the main pillar of your argument will not fall to the ground. But if there be any flaws in this way of arguing if you will point it out to my understanding it will be very acceptable to your humble servant, Eleazer Brooks, Lincoln, Sept. 9, 1771."

The Boston Massacre had recently occurred, the Committees of Correspondence would soon be organized. But for Eleazer the immediate crisis concerned eight or nine members of the Concord Church who had withdrawn in protest against the exclusion of a candidate for membership "believed to be guilty of a certain specified sin that, while unconfessed, was adjudged to be inconsistent with church membership." (The sin is not identified.) These Concord refugees wanted to take communion with the Lincoln congregation. Eleazer Brooks would have none of it. "The Question is whether the Concord Church hath been found guilty upon a legal Trial . . . No such offense hath been found . . . Therefore the aggrieved members cannot be admitted." The fear of dissent and separation, so marked in the days of John Winthrop, is clearly still alive. The church, Eleazer points out, has no Constitution, only "rules of communion with each other." If we depart from those rules, "any persons may break their agreements or covenants at their pleasure." When to his great grief the Lincoln congregation voted to admit the Concord members, Eleazer Brooks and his group put their disapproval officially on record, and Eleazer noted privately that "We . . . consent to their admission only from a spirit of forbearance, hoping that they will ere long be convinced of their duty to return to the Concord church, or that some other door may be opened in Divine Providence . . ." ("If the majority is against them, so much the worse for the majority.")

Concerned as he was with the church, Eleazer never neglected the practical business of running the town. At the time of the fracas over the Concord dissenters, he had served as Town Constable, Surveyor of Highways, Town Treasurer, and Selectman. He had already risen to the rank of captain in the British militia when he resigned his commission to join the American cause. Most important of all, he represented Lincoln in the Massachusetts General Court.

A man of action, Eleazer was also a philosopher. In matters of state he displayed the same sweet and stubborn reasonableness that drove his theological opponents to the wall. Conservative by nature, he considered himself a loyal British subject — within limits. As he declared in the eloquent letter addressed to the Boston Committee of Correspondence, he would fight if he must, but need it come to that? Addressing the General Court, he felt that he was speaking for the people of Lincoln:

"Mr. President. I beg sir to be heard patiently a fiew minutes. I have no inclination to speak much or often; yet being sent here in the capacity of a representative I cannot discharge my duty to my constituents and to my country unless I speak when there is occasion for it and a prospect of doing good . . .

"We sir have some end in view: what is that end? To preserve those rights and liberties which belong to us according to the Laws of God and nature, the English Constitution and the charter of this Province. In what way do we aim to preserve those rights and liberties: by disolving every kind of union with Great Britain and setting up an independent state or by amica[b]ly settling the unhappy controversy occasioned by the unbounded claims of parliament and returning to the same form of government established by our charter?

"The Tories charge us with aiming at the first; we constantly profess the latter; we expressly say that nothing but slavery is more to be dreded than a rupture with Great Britain. . . .

"The Tories tell us to say nothing about our rights but Humbly Petition, and all will be well. We think it best to assert our rights. . . ."

Eleazer Brooks, however, was no firebrand; his fellow townsmen called him "the peacemaker." Rabble-rousers like Sam Adams must have been anathema to him. One can almost hear his calm voice as he continues:

"It is one thing to assert our rights in such a manner as to convey light and demonstration to the rational powers, in such a way as to move the softer passions of the mind (where persons are capable of such passions) in such a manner as to convince our enemies and the world that we are not only firm and resolute but wise and prudent. It is another thing . . . to stir . . . anger, hatred and revenge . . . to give our enemies and Friends and the world reason to think that if we have liberty we shall prove licentious . . ."

If the colonies sincerely want reconciliation with Great Britain, reasons Eleazer, then their leaders should mind their language. He concludes with a bit of homespun philosophy: "Let us reflect a moment on the present state of humane nature. Numberless are the instances that daily happen even in personal cases wherein small differences have been blown up to murder and death by the parties

leaving the merite of the dispute and calling each other
villains, rogues, scoundrels, cowards and a thousand like
words. If that may be the case in small matters, how careful ought we to be in matters of such vast importance as the
dispute between Great Britain and the Colonies."

But it was too late. The humble petitions recommended
by the Tories had been ignored, the harsh words had been
spoken on both sides. In 1773, Eleazer Brooks was chosen
a member of Lincoln's Committee of Correspondence. The
following year he represented the town at the historic meeting of the General Court in Salem, which General Gage
belatedly tried to dissolve, and which reassembled in Concord and later in Cambridge as the Provincial Congress.
When fierce fighting broke out at Concord Bridge, he served
as a private with the rebel forces, though still urging that
the colonists should not fire the first shot. In February
1776, he was commissioned Colonel of the Third Regiment
of Militia in the County of Middlesex; in July his men were
called up "to defend the lines of Fortifications near and
about the Town of Boston."

It was a distinctly local operation; one thinks of the
Daniel Chester French statue of the minuteman leaving his
plow in the field while he goes off to protect his acres. The
men under Brooks — sixty of them from Lincoln — were to
serve only until December 1. Besides their regular pay,
they would receive a penny per mile "in lieu of Rations to
support them on their march going and returning and one
Day's pay for every twenty miles between their Homes and
the general places of Rendezvous."

Friction between the militia and Washington's Continental Army was probably inevitable. When Brooks was given
command of a regiment of guards at Cambridge, despite
his protestations of inexperience in camp service, he was
relieved to learn that a Continental Colonel had been appointed Commandant of the post. This he thought proper,

though it was "looked upon by several gentlemen considerably acquainted in public life to be degrading to the militia." What annoyed him was the way the regular officers avoided taking their tours of duty, pulling their rank but leaving the real work to the militia.

Service in the militia was not necessarily a full-time job, even for the officers. There were, of course, frequent alerts. The colonel would be ordered to see that his regiment was equipped with arms and accoutrements and held "in constant readiness to march at a minute's warning to any place that may be attacked by our Enemies" — be it as nearby as Boston or as far away as Saratoga or West Point. Yet all the while Eleazer kept up with the routine chores of local town government. For the first three years of the war he continued to serve as selectman. In 1777, during the peak period of the fighting in the north, he was also town moderator, a town assessor, and a member of the Committee of Safety. And somehow during this busy spring he found time for more personal concerns. On May 26 he terminated eight years of widowhood by marrying Mrs. Elizabeth Greenough of Boston.

On August 10, 1777, Colonel Brooks received orders from his superior officer, Brigadier General Oliver Prescott, to lead a detachment to Saratoga. It was more than a formal command; Prescott made an eloquent plea that the militia rise to the occasion and show themselves true soldiers. "The state of our military affairs is very alarming . . . The public eye is upon the militia, whose virtue is now loudly called upon, and whose vigorous exertions in the common cause cannot fail, by the blessing of Heaven being crowned with Success and Honour." Only six days later General John Stark would lead his New Hampshire regiment to a spectacular victory over the British and the Hessians at Bennington, Vermont, in what was probably the militia's finest hour. A turning point in the war, the battle of Bennington led to Burgoyne's defeat and surrender at Saratoga — an engagement in which Brooks's regiment presumably took part, and which foiled the enemy's master plan to separate the colonies. The next year Eleazer was named Brigadier General. What probably gave him greater happiness was the birth of his first son, Eleazer Brooks, Jr.

War and peace, state and church, national crisis and local concern blend together in the records of those town meetings over which Eleazer presided as moderator. Six months before the final British surrender at Yorktown, the voters of Lincoln chose two committees: one to hire more men for the army "if need there may be," the other to negotiate with the new Gospel Minister, Mr. Stearns, in respect to his salary. Chairman of the latter was that master of logic and church doctrine, General Brooks. Meanwhile Lincoln's leading citizen was getting more and more involved in state and national affairs. As we have seen, he represented the town at the convention in Cambridge to draw up a new state constitution and criticized the result with characteristic force and eloquence when it came before the town meeting for ratification, largely on the grounds that a small town like Lincoln could be too easily outvoted. When the new state government was established, he was chosen Lincoln's first representative, and was later a state senator. And so when delegates from all over Massachusetts met in Boston in 1788 for the most crucial business of all — the ratification of the Constitution of the United States of America — Eleazer was the obvious choice to speak for Lincoln. We can be sure that he was among those who insisted on the promise of a Bill of Rights to protect individual liberties before he voted aye.

This self-taught farmer from Brooks Village had gone far. No issue seemed too tough for him to tackle. Reading his elaborate criticism of the tax laws, one feels that he was a lawyer manqué; his closely reasoned arguments show the same zeal and confidence that he had previously applied to the dissection of Mr. Lawrence's sermons. During the troubled times of Shays's Rebellion, when the courts of Massachusetts were threatened with violence, he was appointed Special Judge of the Court of Common Pleas and — some years later — Federal Tax Commissioner. Brooks was a firm believer in sound money and the sacredness of property acquired by honest industry. "If we destroy this Idea of Property, all our Ideals of Justice between man and man are at an end." When the so-called Tender Act, designed to relieve the shortage of legal tender, threatened to force creditors to accept goods instead of hard money, Eleazer was indignant. Is it just, he exclaimed, to make a man accept a cow when he needs money to buy a horse? One might as well offer a thirsty man sawdust in lieu of water.

Like the founding fathers, Eleazer Brooks believed that a strong, responsive central government was the only means of preserving individual liberty. "A distinction must be made between a mild and righteous government and a weak and feeble or unsteady government" — which could lead only to despotism. He had the self-taught countryman's distrust of the rich and privileged: "Despotick and absolute government will always court the services of the rich, the learned and the artful part of the people; therefore if a free government is not supported the burden will all fall on the body of the common people and they will have the rich, the learned and the artful for their taskmasters." At the end of the war Eleazer had served on a joint committee of the state legislature to report on the Society of the Cincinnati, the military organization to be composed of male descendants of commissioned officers in the Continental Army. The report damned the scheme on the grounds that such a society, grown rich and powerful and responsible to no civil authority, could be perverted to

evil ends. It might create "an hereditary nobility contrary
to the spirit of all republican government . . . a badge of
distinction between its members and the other citizens."
The Society was nevertheless founded and flourishes today,
and the Republic has survived. But the report, clear and
forthright in its principles, reads as well now as it did when
it came from Eleazer's pen. The words are those of men
brought up in the New England town meeting, where there
are no hereditary badges of distinction and the spirit of republican government is still patently alive.

Eleazer found the State Senate, where he represented
Middlesex County, a very different world from simple, un-
sophisticated Lincoln. Among his papers is a long and un-
characteristically bitter letter of resignation from his Senate seat. Undated, it was apparently written about 1780,
since he refers to his parents as "upwards of eighty-two
years old." Though he was to return later to serve for a
total of nine years, at the moment he felt that he had had
enough. To be sure, he pleaded the necessity of supporting
his aged parents and giving his children, still of tender age,
the attention necessary to keep them on the path of virtue
in a world of sin. "Should they through my neglect acquire
such habits of vice as are at this day become fashionable, it
would be more grievous to me than to see them deposited
in the dust from whence they came." But he obviously had
other reasons for resigning. He was disillusioned and re-
sentful at the way business was conducted. "Unacquainted
with the flattering of courtiers, I have attended to the more
plain and simple dictates of nature and reason . . . I have
at no time used any other endeavors to get myself promoted
to places of honour or profit . . . I have always supposed
that the Court as a Court meant to do right; I heartily wish
that I could say the same for every individual."

Eleazer regrets his lack of a liberal education and wishes
that there were more men of learning in the seats of gov-

ernment. But learning has its dangers: "It is too often seen that a speech will carry all before it . . . merely on account of its beautiful ornaments when it scarcely contains statements of common sense." Something had gone wrong. "I see nothing to tempt an honest man to continue in the General Court, except the having an opportunity to contribute something to the public good . . . But he no sooner begins to realize even an honorary reward but he finds himself the butt of envy and disappointed ambitions and is in danger of falling a sacrifice to such baser passion unless he puts forth such exertions of his own as seem inconsistent with the principles of honor and modesty . . ." Never a man of few words, Eleazer ends his letter with a parting shot: "When this my resignation shall be thrown among other waste papers, and I shall have returned to private life, I shall suppose that the wheels of government are moving as usual, and that while some are making it their main design and endeavour to act for the public good, others are using artifice and low cunning to procure to themselves and their connections places of honor and profit. That the former may be succeeded [i.e., succeed] and the latter bested or reformed is the sincere wish and prayer of your obedient servant Eleazer Brooks."

In spite of Eleazer's lifelong devotion to public affairs, he was never divorced from the land. In his later years, as his public responsibilities grew lighter, he had more time for his farm, and at the age of sixty-five joined the Massachusetts Society for the Promotion of Agriculture. Small diversified farms such as the one on Brooks Road that Eleazer inherited from his forebears, with its plowland and pasture, its orchard and meadow, its woodlot and cedar swamp, have all but vanished. Yet the attitude toward the land that these first settlers brought with them from the mother country, the sense of stewardship rather than exploitation, has survived, to be reborn as the best means of maintaining the quality of life in an industrial age. Together with the tradition of public service, they make Lincoln what it is today.

Not till the age of seventy-five did Eleazer decline all public office and retire completely to his farm. There he died on November 9, 1806, at the age of seventy-nine. Lincoln itself was over fifty years old, in many ways a typical New England town, but with its own character and personality. The pattern was set. Though growth and change were inevitable, they would come slowly during the ensuing century. The small farms would endure. The same families, generation after generation, would be deacons in the church, "town fathers" in the civil government. The one dramatic moment in history — the trial by fire — would never be repeated. When change at last did come, after almost two centuries, with the growth of the suburbs and the end of the farms, the supreme importance of the past, the value of attitudes and institutions going back to the days of Eleazer Brooks, became immediately apparent. No amount of urban sprawl, no pressure of migration from the city, could transform Lincoln into just another suburb. In the deepest sense of the term, Lincoln was and is a town.

A Living Tradition

CHAPTER 10 ⌐

"The New Englander is attached to his Township not so much because he was born in it, but because it is a free and strong community, of which he is a member, and which deserves the care spent in managing it."
— Alexis de Tocqueville, *Democracy in America,* 1835

Back to Beginnings

As a New Englander concerned with land conservation, I occasionally find myself at odds with colleagues from the West. We all agree that our rural and suburban communities must somehow be defended against ruthless exploitation and unplanned urban sprawl. We agree on the need for federal and state legislation. The westerners, however, tend to distrust local town government and would reduce its power in favor of the state. What they ignore, in urging such a policy across the board, is the impressive record in land use of that ancient organization, the New England town.

Look down from the air at the megalopolis that spreads like a fungus along the Atlantic seaboard, or drive through bulldozer subdivisions and shopping plazas and across polluted rivers, and you will find it hard to believe that the first settlement of New England was an early example of what we would now call planned development. Look closer and you will see that patterns of land use established centuries ago are still discernible and that a long tradition of controlled growth has not wholly lost its power. Many New England towns, even near the great cities, still enhance the beauty and meaning of the landscape. Where did this tradition come from? Surely it is rooted in that sense of community which the first settlers brought with them from their native villages in England and which, through years of precarious survival in the wilderness where they had no one to rely on except themselves, evolved into a very different relation of man to the land from that of landlord and peasant in the old country. If, as historians have pointed out, the New England colonists were peculiarly successful in coming to terms with their environment, one obvious reason is the disciplined orderly way in which they ran their affairs.

There is a mystique associated with the New England town that invites romantic, far-out theories to explain its origin. Nineteenth-century scholars carried on a lively debate on the subject in the learned journals, their imagination and ingenuity given free rein by the lack of documentary evidence. American democracy, as represented in the New England town meeting, was seen as the daughter of democracy in Athens — or, going back further, somehow related to the Homeric *agora*. Lincoln's selectmen today, slogging through their endless agenda as the village clock strikes the hour of midnight, might comfort themselves with more than apples if they recalled the words of one of these historians: "Seen from within, these New England towns and villages are as full today of youthful freshness, quiet beauty, and energetic life as the *demes* of Grecian Attika, in the springtime of the world."

Other scholars, somewhat more realistically, traced the origins of our town government to prototypes in England. But unwilling to stop there, they looked back to the savage peoples of the Germanic forests, whose fierce independence not even the Roman legions could conquer. "Upon the forest hill-tops they worshipped Wodan, the All Father; in the forest valleys they talked over, in village-moot, the lowly affairs of husbandry and management of their common fields. Here were planted the seeds of . . . self-government . . . that formed . . . England and New England."

Perhaps. It would be nice to think that the spirit of Wodan still looks down upon our deliberations on Lincoln Hill.

Seeking a continental European origin for our local political system, other writers tried to establish a link with the Swiss cantons of the sixteenth century. During the reign of "Bloody Mary," so the theory goes, many prominent English Protestants took refuge in Switzerland, where they formed their own congregations on the pattern of the cantons; and when they returned home after the accession of Queen Elizabeth, they brought with them an intimate knowledge of the Swiss system of democratic local government. The fact is, however, that there is no need to go as far as Switzerland. Modern scholars point to the overwhelming tradition in England of local self-government in village and borough, a tradition that at the local level was democratic. And that it is fundamentally English is clear from the names of town officials, directly carried over to New England from the mother country.

But what about religious origins? Most of us were brought up on the idea that New England town government was a direct outgrowth of, and at first identical with, the Puritan Congregational Church. Certainly the clergy, together with the magistrates, formed the ruling class in the Colony. On the other hand, the original charter set up a corporation on the lines of a joint stock company: the freemen were the stockholders; the magistrates the directors; the governor the president; and so on. The obvious conclusion is that towns, like people, have a complex genetic inheritance. In New England the church was of course central; in early seventeenth-century England the terms "town" and "parish" were interchangeable. Nevertheless, the Massachusetts Bay Company was chartered as a commercial venture. In his *Magnalia Christi Americana*, Cotton Mather tells of a preacher who admonished his parishioners to be religious "otherwise they would contradict the main end of planting this wilderness." A prominent citizen interrupted him: "Sir, you are mistaken . . . our main end was to catch fish."

The charter itself gave political power to the "freemen," who had to be church members: not merely churchgoers, but communicants who had been formally accepted into the church. Only they could serve as town officers, admit new inhabitants, allot land. Only they could vote on issues concerning the Colony as a whole. Yet any resident could attend town meeting and vote upon local matters. As early as 1641 the Body of Liberties provided that "Every man whether Inhabitant or fforreiner, free or not free shall have libertie to come to any . . . Towne meeting and . . . to move any lawful, seasonable, and material question. . ." Six years later the General Court, "taking into consideration the useful partes and abilities of divers inhabitants amongst us, which are not freemen," extended the vote in local affairs to all qualified inhabitants who had reached the age of twenty-four and required only that a majority of the Selectmen be freemen.

Although church and town were not synonymous, they consisted of generally the same persons, gathered together — during the early years — in the same building. Though for religious service pews were assigned according to wealth or rank, at town meeting, then as now, it was a matter of first come, first served. Town meetings were, however, deeply involved in church matters, including the selection of a minister and the payment of his salary. (Under the laws of the Colony the clergy could not hold town office.) As we have seen, Lincoln itself came into being in large part because of the need for a more conveniently located place of worship; its evolution from a district to a precinct to a town shows how an independent religious congregation develops into a political unit. But local politics were also involved. Would Chambers Russell have pushed so hard to create Lincoln if Concord had built a road to his estate?

Neither church nor state represented what one could call true "democracy," a word little used in the seventeenth century, and then not as a term of approval.* From the beginning social position and personal fortune were recognized in the choice of leaders. John Winthrop was a country gentleman and justice of the peace — a member of the ruling class, as were most of the early magistrates. In 1670 the General Court narrowed the franchise by requiring that voters (unless already on the rolls) must, in addition to being church members, own a taxable estate of not less than eighty pounds — thus excluding many younger men and the less affluent among new citizens. How far the franchise actually extended, just how much "democracy" really existed, is a subject on which leading authorities take diametrically opposite views. Apparently freemen were in the majority during those final decades of the Puritan supremacy before Massachusetts became a royal province. Sad to relate, however, many colonists who could have been freemen declined the honor in order to avoid the irksome duties involved. Thus the rich and well-born were not always freemen; the humble and poor sometimes were. In her study of "Freemanship in Puritan Massachusetts," B. Katherine Brown notes that in 1647 the General Court, having officially declared a certain Mighill Smith to be a freeman, was then obliged to fine him "for his putin in of three beanes at once for a man's election." The Court then went on to suspend the sentence on the grounds of "it being done in simplicity, and he being pore and of a harmless disposition." Mighill was clearly neither rich nor well-born.

Whatever the criteria for full citizenship may have been, an official policy of exclusiveness was taken for granted.

* In defending the power of the magistrates, John Winthrop wrote that "a Democratie is, among most civil nations, accounted the meanest and worst of all forms of government." John Cotton agreed: "Democracy I do not conceive that God ever did ordain as a fit government for either church or commonwealth. . .   He setteth up theocracy. . .as the best form of government in the commonwealth as in the church."

For example, Dedham, Massachusetts, in the words of historian Kenneth A. Lockridge, was originally a "Christian Utopian Closed Corporate Community." The founders began by signing a Covenant. "The select group of townsmen and their perpetually committed descendants would then live under the rules of the Covenant, the land theirs to assign, their rare disputes contained within the town. . . A townsman signing the Covenant incurred an obligation to tell whatever he might know about future candidates for admission. Every candidate would undergo a public inquisition in which his entire past could be brought to light." Granted this was an extreme case, the records of the Bay Colony reflect a tradition of close control, the very opposite of liberalism.

Some years ago, when "Puritan" was widely used as a term of opprobrium, the first settlers on Massachusetts Bay were frequently accused of being hypocrites because they left England under the banner of liberty and then promptly clamped down on dissenters when they themselves were in the saddle. But as Professor Morison has pointed out, the connection between puritanism and liberalism was largely fortuitous: "English puritans in 1630 rallied to representative government and traditional English liberty be-

cause that was their only refuge against innovating Bishops and a high church King; but in New England where they had things their own way, their political spirit was conservative and their temper autocratic." However, the Puritan village, whose imprint still lies on New England, represents a passionate dedication to an ideal, a deep sense of participation in a common cause.

From the start, a principal concern of the Bay Colony leaders was land planning. The frontier cliché of land for the taking did not apply here. Though there were a number of scattered settlements in the Bay area before Governor Winthrop and his party arrived aboard the *Arbella* in 1630, one of the first acts of the Court of Assistants was to forbid further indiscriminate settlement. Only the General Court might dispose of land; only the magistrates might regulate "the sitting downe of men in any newe plantation." In the course of an elaborate defense of this policy, Winthrop expresses in simple terms how the colonists felt toward each other and toward the world outside: "A family is a little common wealth, and a common wealth is a greate family. Now as a family is not bound to entertaine all comers, no not every good man (otherwise than by way of hospitality) no more is a common wealth." The Puritans, however, cannot be accused of "snob-zoning" in an economic sense. As Winthrop's contemporary, Edward Johnson, points out in his *Wonder-Working Providence*, the Selectmen of Woburn "refused not men for their poverty, but according to their ability were helpful to the poorest sort, in building their houses, and distributed them land accordingly." Nevertheless, in this close-knit community, the residents were expected to behave themselves. "Such as were exhorbitant, and of a Turbulent spirit, unfit for civil society, they would reject, till they come to mend their manners."

The vital role of the town in controlling the use of land, characteristic of New England, goes back to the original policy of the General Court in making initial land grants not to individuals but to an organized group, to the town itself. This was in sharp contrast to the practice in the colony of Virginia, and of course to the later practice of the federal government in settling the West. The system by which the town parceled out the land to the settlers according to their needs, for their personal improvement, discouraged the accumulation of large land fortunes. Speculation was further prevented by the provision that owners wishing to sell their plots or their "individual rights" in the common land must first offer them to the town, which meant no stranger could buy them without the town's consent. We can be thankful that the men of Massachusetts Bay set up such controls as one of their first acts. Otherwise, considering the speed with which the Colony grew, our predecessors might have contracted an early and incurable case of urban sprawl. In 1630 alone seventeen ships deposited about one thousand settlers in the Bay area. This was only the beginning of the so-called Great Migration from England, during the despotic rule of Charles I and Archbishop Laud, which within a single decade brought the population of New England to almost twenty thousand.

Though New England towns differed in the procedures for land development, depending on the varying local traditions that the first settlers brought with them from different parts of England, the usual pattern was that of the "open-field village": a main street with closely placed dwellings on relatively small house lots, each owner having his share of tillage beyond, as well as his rights in the meadows, pastureland, and woods that were held in common. We have seen that Concord started this way, but here as elsewhere holdings had to be consolidated for practical purposes of farming. Lincoln of course was founded long after the "nuclear village" concept had been abandoned and farmers were living on their own land. Inevitably this dispersion limited daily communication with neighbors and strengthened the influence of the family unit. And since the first division of land had been made on the basis of wealth and rank, and subsequent divisions were based on the acreage already owned, it paid to be a pioneer; for many generations a large proportion of the land was held by relatively few families. These are the families whose names appear again and again, in one official capacity or another, in town and church records down almost to the present day. At Lincoln's hundred-and-fiftieth anniversary celebration in 1904, Charles Francis Adams remarked that the officers chosen when the precinct was founded in 1746 might, judging from their patronymics, "have been selected yesterday."

As population grew, some machinery other than the town meeting itself was obviously essential for implementing the individual town governments. The problem was acute in Charlestown from the earliest days. "By reason of many men meeting, things were not so easily brought into a joint issue." A committee was appointed "to be at town meetings to assist in ordering their affairs." Soon afterward the first Board of Selectmen was officially established to carry on the town's business between meetings. So with the other settlements, each however having its own variations. Later the burden of administration would be divided among various town officers, but at first the Selectmen had the whole job to do themselves. They assessed land, set tax rates, paid the minister, oversaw the fences, protected the timber in the commons, and ordered "the Ringeinge and yonkeinge [yoking] of Hogges." No wonder that in these early days some towns had ten or more Selectmen. To quote a recent study of town government in Massachusetts, "the Selectmen were, as they still remain, the 'first men' of the community, held to an exacting responsibility that only the public criticism of neighbors can compel. A recital of their powers rings with the broad finality of dictatorship in local matters, but the spirit of their service resembles the humblest agent."

One office which anteceded even that of Selectman was Town Constable. Traditionally, New England's first Constable was that schoolbook hero, Plymouth's Miles Standish. In the Bay Colony the Constable was a key figure. Then as now, it was his duty to notify voters of town meeting. In former times he also had charge of highways, levied fines, apprehended Quakers, and was supposed to "attend funerals of any, that die of the small pox, and walk before the corpse to give notice to any, who may be in danger of the infection." As the town grew, he was given the distasteful duty of warning out of town those families or individuals who threatened to become a financial burden on the community. But his most arduous job was that of tax collector. He was held personally responsible for collection; if he failed to obtain all that was due, he was obliged to make up the difference. No wonder the office was unpopular. Once elected, however, the unfortunate townsman had to serve or pay a fine. Many chose the fine; the Concord records, for example, show one man after another declining until at last someone was found willing to take the job — or more likely unable to afford the alternative. As late as 1754, the year that Lincoln was founded, the Concord town meeting voted down a proposal to choose tax collectors separate from Constables, and went on to refuse extra pay to last year's Constables for "extraordinary service." Yet apparently no one objected to an appropriation in the Treasurer's report for "Rum to entertain Selectmen."

A few years after the colonies had won their independence, the Massachusetts legislature passed its first general act "for regulating Towns, setting forth their Power, and for the Choice of Town-Officers." The act of 1786 confirmed the procedures already in effect. Each town was to elect a Moderator, a Clerk, and "three, five, seven or nine able and discreet persons of good conversation to be Selectmen or Townsmen." In addition there were to be a Treasurer, three or more Assessors, two or more Fence Viewers, Surveyors of Highways, Surveyors of Lumber, Wardens, Tithingmen, "and other usual town officers" — including of course the Constable, who summoned those chosen to take oath of office before the Town Clerk.*

For its first thirty-six years, Lincoln had five Selectmen; thereafter the number was three. For many years the Selectmen customarily — though not always — served also as Assessors, and beginning in the 1820s, as Overseers of the Poor. Their statutory duties, under state law, also included calling town meetings, appointing certain officials, laying out roads, running the town boundary lines, and (though Lincoln records are unenlightening here) granting liquor licenses and posting the names of any "common drunkards, common tipplers, or common gamesters who are misspending their time and estate, ruining their health and threatening to become a charge on the town."

In Lincoln, both Treasurer and Collector (which was eventually separated from the office of Constable) were paid jobs; they were auctioned off to the lowest bidder. At first the Treasurer took a percentage of the money he handled. When he was lucky he would get twopence on the pound, but one year the low bidder, who must have been hard up for a job, took it for a penny. In later years, aspirants for Town Treasurer bid a flat sum; in 1840, for example, the office was "knocked off to Charles Wheeler, Esq., at six dollars." Collectors continued to take a cut of the taxes they collected; that same year this office was "knocked off" to Edmond Wheeler for one cent, one mill on the dol-

* A recent Lincoln Town Clerk, who served for thirty-six years and knew most residents by voice as well as by sight, had the convenient custom of administering the oath of office by telephone, as the citizen at the other end of the wire solemnly raised his right hand.

lar. Though Collectors were occasionally voted extra pay
for their "extraordinary services," tax delinquency became
an ever more acute problem, to the point where the town
felt obliged to require a bond of the Collector to assure that
he would deliver on time. One such town meeting vote
was made the occasion for a homily on the injury that delinquency was inflicting on "those inhabitants who nobly
exert themselves to pay their taxes in season" as well as on
"the delinquents themselves by encouraging, through expectation of long indulgence, to dispose of each part of their
property as might be spared for the payment of their taxes,
for unnecessary, and in many instances for very bad purposes."

In terms of physical labor, upkeep of roads was the big-
gest communal responsibility; in Lincoln's first century,
the number of Surveyors of Highways grew from four to
fourteen. Residents worked off their road tax at the rate of
about four shillings a day. An average annual appropriation for roadwork would be forty pounds — two hundred
man-days. Strict accounts were kept: "If any person shall
neglect or refuse to work out the sum . . . which he or she
[did the women work too?] shall be assessed," the balance
was added to his tax bill. Yet the town itself frequently
neglected repair of county roads, such as North Great Road
of Revolutionary fame, and had to defend itself against
suits to force compliance.

Though major positions — Selectman, Moderator, Town
Clerk, Treasurer — have endured, minor offices changed
with the passing years. Those endemic to a frontier or
purely rural community have disappeared, except as honorary, half-humorous gestures. The titles of Measurer of
Wood and Bark, which once entailed inspection of all firewood put up for sale, or of Fence Viewer, which involved
Solomon-like judgments of neighbors' disputes about upkeep of fences, are now bestowed on some young man re-

cently married, or upon a Selectman or other town official
on retirement from office, as a token of affection and esteem.
Many traditional titles that date from the Middle Ages
have gone forever. Deer Reeves are no longer needed to
protect growing crops; now we have only Dog Officers. It
is many years since Hog Reeves were required to see that
swine were "sufficiently yoked," in order not to slip through
fences when they were allowed to go at large.* The Field
Drivers have also vanished. They originally got their name
from their duty of protecting the common fields against un-
authorized grazing; later they impounded any stray beasts,
including any ungelded horse or any ram or he-goat that
shall "be out of his inclosure between the tenth of August
and the twentieth of November." "As early as 1668,"
writes Professor Morison, "the Massachusetts general court
took measures to improve the breed [of horses] by allowing only stallions 'of comely proportions and fourteen
hands in stature' to run free on the town common."

Other early town offices have disappeared. Surveyors of
Lumber went out with the sawmills — of which Lincoln
once had an abundance. Similar casualties are Sealer of
Weights and Measures, who made an annual checkup of
merchants and shopkeepers, and Sealer of Leather — though
Lincoln, perhaps because of its active tannery, continued to
appoint such an official after this was no longer required by
the state, which allowed each manufacturer to stamp his
own products, including boots, half-boots, shoes, pumps,
sandals, slippers, and "goloshoes." One traditional position
might — in view of the present Sunday traffic on the highways — be profitably revived. The Tithingmen were
charged not only with apprehending idle and disorderly
persons, profane swearers and cursers, and Sabbath-break-

* Beginning in 1715, Concord required that every man married in town
during the year be chosen "to observe the law relating to swine" — i.e., to
serve as Hog Reeve. What effect this had on the marriage rate has not been
determined.

ers; they might also fine anyone found guilty of unnecessary traveling on the Lord's day.

As Lincoln entered the modern age, a host of new offices grew up, hydra-like, in place of those that had been cut off. The duties originally performed by the Selectmen and the Town Constable are now scattered among a score of boards and committees, some of which would surely have puzzled early Lincolnians. They might well have foreseen the need, as the town grew, for Water Commissioners, a Board of Health, a Building Inspector, a Cemetery Commission. But what would they have made of "Plumbing Inspector"? Or of "Representative to Subregion Intertown Liaison Committee"?

Two present town boards, both relatively young, would not have seemed strange to them at all. The Planning Board and the Conservation Commission, wrestling with the problems of the population explosion in the gasoline age, are dealing in modern terms with a matter that concerned the colonists from the very start: the use of the land. As early as the first decade of the Bay Colony, individual towns were limiting the admission of "foreigners" to avoid what they considered overpopulation. And year after year the records show how much thought was devoted to the physical development of the community: to the proper location of roads and byways, to the siting of public buildings, to the upkeep of highways and bridges and fences and stone walls. No detail was too small for public consideration at town meeting. When in 1790 a new road was being laid out in Lincoln through the property of the Pierce family, it was to be done "in some way and manner by which the said Jonas Pierce and Jacob his son may have the privilege of a certain spring of water." Again, when five years later John Adams wanted to move the west wall of the burying yard "even with the middle of the East stone at the Gateway of the Pound," he was given permission provided that he made the wall four and a half feet high and "faced as well as may be with such like stones as is at present in the Wall." These men would not have been surprised, could they have looked a century and a half into the future, to see the Chairman of the Planning Board out early one morning with his surveyor's tape to determine what trees could be saved when the road over Lincoln Hill had to be widened and the stone wall rebuilt.

Like all suburban towns, Lincoln has grown to the point where no one can hope to know every fellow townsman, or to keep up with the work of every board and committee. But personal pride in community endures. Inherited from the past, continually shaping the future, is a tradition of public service, of participation in the chores of local government. A substantial part of the population is involved at one time or another in managing the town's daily affairs and planning for decades ahead. These year-round activities tend to reach a frenetic climax early in the new year. About the time that the groundhog traditionally emerges to look for his shadow, the voters of Lincoln and hundreds of other New England towns begin looking forward to the salutary ordeal that holds the whole thing together — the annual town meeting.

CHAPTER 11 ⌟

"Town meetings are to liberty what primary schools are to
science: they bring it within the people's reach, they teach men
how to use and how to enjoy it."
— Alexis de Tocqueville

"Town Meeting To Day Makes a great nois and hubbub."
— Theodore Foster, Brookfield, 1768

Town Meeting Tonight

"COMMONWEALTH OF MASSACHUSETTS
MIDDLESEX S.S.
To either of the Constables of the Town of Lincoln in said County:
"GREETING:
In the name of the Commonwealth you are hereby required to notify the legal voters of said Town of Lincoln qualified to vote in Town Meeting for the Transaction of Town affairs to meet in the Brooks School Auditorium in said Lincoln . . ."

It is late March and the sun is just crossing the equator on its journey north; by early evening dusk will have fallen over New England. West of Lincoln Hill, a double necklace of slowly moving lights converges toward the level ground of the modern school complex, now and then illuminating a sign on a roadside tree: "TOWN MEETING TONIGHT."*

---

* In 1971 the time of the annual town meeting was changed from Monday evening to Saturday morning, allowing a full day for its deliberations, and making less likely the need for a second or even third session. Special meetings are still held on Monday evenings. In earlier times, before anyone went out of town to work, all meetings were held during daylight hours.

Some years ago the number of legal voters outgrew the "new town hall," dedicated so proudly on that May morning of 1892. For a while, the school gymnasium had to serve for town meetings. Now a spacious, well-appointed auditorium provides a setting for our deliberations such as Lincoln's founders, in their bare, unheated meetinghouse, could never have conceived in their wildest and most sinful dreams of earthly comfort. Even in the short view, things have changed. Those of us who still associate town meeting with the square raftered room of the upper town hall, with its long rows of attached wooden chairs and its balcony for non-voters, already look back with nostalgia to the pre-microphone era when you could stand up in your place and be heard. But as for the deliberations themselves, even those hardy men (no women, of course) of 1754 would have found these familiar enough — if not in substance, certainly in spirit.

"A description of town meeting government is the despair of the expert," writes a New England historian, "but as a 'going' concern there is a long record of sustained accomplishment that newer devices of democracy have too often failed to equal." This is not to claim that the New England town meeting is the principal source of our democratic political system, which has taken shape in an urban, industrialized society. Yet as one scans the early records, the conventional phrase "school of democracy" seems amply justified.

The annual meeting was, and still is, held in March. In former times when state officials were elected annually, the laws of the Commonwealth also required a meeting on the first Monday in April to elect the Governor, Lieutenant-Governor, and State Senators; in May to elect a Representative to the General Court; and on the first Monday in November to elect a Representative in the United States Congress. There were two classes of voters: "Inhabitants of the town who were duly qualified to vote for a Governor, etc.," (sometimes referred to as "freeholders") and "Inhabitants . . . qualified to vote in town affairs." The first class consisted of citizens who had paid a state or county tax during the preceding year, the second of all property owners in town.* April, May, and November meetings required for state elections were immediately followed by technically separate meetings devoted to town business, of which there was always more than the annual meeting could anticipate or encompass.

Year after year, the appropriations voted at town meetings, together with payments made by the Town Treasurer, give us a pretty good idea of what the citizens considered most essential to the welfare of the community. Let us look at the record for Concord during the year that Lincoln was born. Concord, in 1754, had already experienced more than a century of self-government and the pattern of life was well established.

That year, as usual, a major item was the upkeep of the highways. With roads went bridges. The annual town meeting voted to rebuild "Great South Bridge" over the Sudbury River and to pay Captain Charles Prescott for "Poles for Bridge" — this being the North Bridge then a-building, and soon to echo to "the shot heard round the

* Though social distinctions were also recognized, they seem to have had little influence on how men voted in town affairs. Some were gentlemen entitled to a "Mr." before or an "Esq." after their names; most were farmers — and the latter apparently had no hesitation in voting down pet projects of the former. At least this was true by Chambers Russell's day. Though he represented Concord in the General Court, he sometimes failed to get his way at home, in other matters as well as in the separation of Lincoln. Less than a year after he had been chosen both Selectman and Town Representative, the Town Treasurer reported payment "for measuring ways in order to opose the granting of Mr. Chambers Russels petition" for a bridge across the Concord River at "Sandy Point." To be sure, he eventually won out; a later report lists payments to surveyors and chainmen, "which money was the produce of the Sale of Common Land." It is interesting to note that, after more than a century, the sale of undistributed land was still an important source of financing town projects.

world." Five years later a town lottery was authorized to
pay for its completion.

From the beginning, schools were an important concern,
though they absorbed nowhere near the proportion of town
revenues that they do today. In Concord in 1754, forty
pounds sufficed to keep "Grammar School at the School
House," as well as four "out schoolls" (presumably in private houses) for the year. Three hundred bricks were purchased to mend the schoolhouse, and a new schoolhouse was
planned in the southeast corner of town, soon to become a
part of Lincoln.

The minister's salary was, of course, a major item. Money
was also appropriated annually for indigent widows and
for the poor. ". . . for moving the Widow Ruth Pike from
the House of the widow Buss with her Goods, Two Shillings
and Eight pence . . ." At this time, a private house was
being rented for an alms- or workhouse, but a committee
was appointed to consider building one for the town. Concern that it should not become overcrowded is suggested by
the payments made to the Town Constables for warning
six families, as well as a mother and daughter and single
woman, out of town, lest they become a financial burden
on the community.

Though town planning boards and building inspectors
were still far in the future, certain items discussed at town
meeting that year have a familiar ring in their attention to
detail of planning and construction. Should permission be
given to build a stable "by the Side of the Burying place"?
Or to move the Town Pound five feet? Permission for the
latter was granted "on condition of underpinning it properly with stones when it is Removed." The customary vote
that "Swine shall have liberty to go at Large within the
Towne the Ensuing Year" assured that the Hog Reeves
would not lack for business in keeping them under control.

Such were the routine measures of an average year. As

we have seen, the warrant for the Concord annual meeting on March 4, 1754, contained one highly controversial article that must have overshadowed all the others: an article to create the town of Lincoln. After long debate it had been "passed over," but Chambers Russell achieved the same end some six weeks later by direct appeal to the General Court.

*   *   *

Following its incorporation in April, Lincoln had held a series of town meetings during this first year of its official existence, most of them necessarily concerned with organization. Of course the residents were already off to a running start, having enjoyed their own precinct for the previous eight years. They had their meetinghouse and their minister and their burying place, and they were used to working together under their chosen leaders. The Honorable Chambers Russell, Esq., was elected Moderator and shortly thereafter was chosen to be Lincoln's Representative in the General Court. The posts of Town Clerk and Treasurer were both filled by Mr. Ephraim Flint (whose daughter, the future Mary Hartwell, would one day watch the British Regulars march by her door). He was also one of five Selectmen. Among the first decisions was that to keep a school in "three several places" and to provide a schoolmaster. Road repair was also high on the list, then at the rate of only one shilling and eightpence for an eight-hour day. Jurors had to be selected and certain other matters respecting the Colony as a whole had to be dealt with, such as the excise tax on wines and spirits. But Lincoln was from the start, and for many years would remain, a simple farming community, obligated to work with its neighboring towns — as for example in maintaining the bridges over the Sudbury River — but essentially concerned with its own fifteen square miles of earth.

By today's standards, the warrant for the annual Lincoln

town meeting during the eighteenth and nineteenth centuries was blissfully short, generally consisting of six to ten articles. Most of these were recurrent items, similar to those in all New England towns: election of town officers, appointment of a committee to examine the Treasurer's accounts, upkeep of highways and bridges, road takings, the minister's salary (paid partly in firewood), repairs on the meetinghouse, appropriations for schools and support of the poor. In most years Lincoln needed at least one meeting, in addition to those required by law, for transaction of local business. This was usually held in midsummer or early fall.

Not all was routine. There were bound to be occasional acts of obstreperousness on the part of Lincoln residents sufficiently serious to merit disciplinary action at town meeting. Thus the article: "To bring to punishment those persons, who did of late on a public Fast Day, irregularly ring the town bell without order, and out of season, greatly to the disturbance of the peace and order of the Church and congregation, in this town." More serious was the delivery one Sabbath morning to Dr. Stearns at the meetinghouse door of a letter to be read, as the custom was, to the congregation, the contents of which turned out to be "such as to amount to a public insult . . . upon their Rev. and worthy Pastor . . . upon the town . . . upon Religion and its divine Author . . . for which conduct they entertain the highest Detestation and Abhorrence . . ." and so on for half a page of the town records. It must have been quite a letter.

Such incidents were the exception. Occasionally town officers had to use force to carry out their decrees, as for instance in evicting squatters from a house the town owned and wanted to rent: "Voted to direct the constable to clear the Baker House of its present incumbents, and to nail up said House." Not all taxpayers were honest; the town had to deal with "Fraud and deception of Cyrus Brown for having refused and neglected to give in a true and correct Invoice of his Personal property when legally called upon by the assessors." Gullible but doubtless innocent was another citizen who paid his taxes with a counterfeit eight-dollar bill.

Personal problems would occasionally come before the meeting. Though the town government was paternalistic to a degree that we should never tolerate today, by the same token it would assume a responsibility for individuals that is difficult in a larger community. Often this was a matter of financial support, apparently in addition to the annual appropriation made for the poor. The citizens would, for example, undertake the maintenance of a child "thrown upon the town." In one case when a resident died leaving his "reputed daughter" penniless, the town requisitioned part of his estate for her support. In another case, it collected an unpaid doctor's bill under similar circumstances. Some of the early votes are tantalizingly shrouded in the mists of time. One would like to know just how the distinguished committee headed by Eleazer Brooks decided "to settle with the Honorable James Russell, Esq., with respect to his servant Bacchus Child," and to know how the latter — presumably black — got his name.

Concerned though they were with neighborhood matters, Lincoln town meetings, as we have seen in the Revolutionary years, were ready with strong opinions and eloquent words when some state or national issue was at stake. They took pride in their patriotism and their independence. Witness the resolution passed on February 14, 1809, supporting Thomas Jefferson in maintenance of the embargo that was imposed on trade with Great Britain and France, in retaliation for impressment of sailors and depredations on American shipping. Perhaps because they were farmers rather than merchants, the men of Lincoln refused to join in the howl of protest against the embargo that had arisen along the New England seaboard; on the contrary, they strongly opposed interference by the state legislature and proclaimed themselves convinced of the necessity of obeying the law and supporting the national government of their choice. (Five years earlier they had voted almost four to one for Jefferson.) They deplored the barrage of resolutions from New England town meetings denouncing those who obeyed the Embargo Act: "Such Resolutions may produce Riots and Insurrections, but in our minds [they produce] a determination to rally round the Government chosen by the Majority of the People. . . We place so much confidence in our National Government, as to believe the Embargo Laws will be repealed as soon as the honour and interest of our Country will permit. . ." It was a sound prediction; the Embargo Act, which had hurt America rather than its enemies, was repealed a month later.

In the course of over two centuries of Lincoln history, such involvements in national affairs are rare, but they are significant in suggesting how the New England town meeting trained men in debate, how it developed a political cast of mind and an independence of thought that, spreading beyond New England's border, would accompany the covered wagons to the shores of the Pacific. In that sense it was and is a school of democracy.

*   *   *

7:30 P.M. "The Meeting will come to order . . ." Latecomers are still hurrying down the aisles, hands full of the book-length annual town report, the supplement containing both the financial section and the warrant (the list of articles for the meeting), and likely as not several multigraphed pages and maps that were handed them at the door, as technical background for some complicated article to be considered. Standing on the stage before a microphone, the Town Clerk seated at his side, the Moderator does not have to raise his voice: his patience, not his vocal cords, will likely suffer strain before the night is out. Demanding constant alertness, requiring both courtesy and firmness, his is the key role that sets the tone of the meeting. Though he must know, and in general must follow, the rules of parliamentary procedure, the law gives him great freedom of action. The courts have ruled that "judicially the town meeting is not a representative body, but a pure democracy. . . The technical rules of parliamentary law. . . are in some respects ill adapted for the transaction of [its] affairs." Rarely does a citizen revolt against the Moderator's ruling. Those who do insist on talking out of turn might well recall the statute of 1786 that gives the Moderator power to put such persons "into the stocks, cage, or some other place of confinement, and there be detained for three hours, unless the Town-meeting shall sooner adjourn or dissolve." There are times when one cannot help wishing that this power, presumably still valid, were more freely exercised.

Below the Moderator, at long tables facing the assembled company, are the "town fathers" (of both sexes): the Selectmen, the Town Treasurer, the Finance Committee, the School Committee, the Board of Health, the Planning Board . . .

The first group of routine articles (including provision for later balloting on elective offices) is disposed of quickly, except for certain items in the appropriations article that are "held out" for separate discussion, which may go on indefinitely. Then comes the long list of articles beginning: "To see if* the Town will . . ." Many of these are also routine, or noncontroversial. An outside observer might guess that everything would be over in an hour or two. Not so. Here comes the big one we have all been waiting for.

---

* In misguided pursuit of elegance, someone changed "To see if" in 1956 to "To determine whether." The traditional form was restored in 1970.

Papers rustle, feet shuffle, as the sponsoring officials get out their notes and the opposition limbers up its verbal artillery. The school of democracy is in session.

When the House of Commons was rebuilt after the bombings of World War II, Winston Churchill insisted that the size remain the same (better a crowded hall at dramatic moments than routine empty seats) and that the floor plan remain unaltered: two tiers of benches facing each other, one for the Government and one for the Opposition, leaving no doubt as to which side any member was on. In our Senate and House, Republicans and Democrats sit on either side of the aisle. In Lincoln town meeting, however, one sits anywhere, because national party affiliations have never counted here. Each issue is decided on its local merits. Yet this apparently simple system has depths and subtleties that newcomers may not appreciate until they have lived with it awhile.

As in the national Congress, it is the committees, the boards, the officials who do the work. An article in the warrant represents only the tip of the iceberg. Out of sight, and so likely to be forgotten, are weeks and months of study, deliberations far into the night, dedication of volunteer time and talent that the richest town could never afford to buy. On critical issues there may have been local meetings in various parts of town to answer questions in detail. A week before the official date, the League of Women Voters will have held a "pre-town meeting" to explain difficult articles in advance and to give candidates for office a chance to present their views.

Without such preparation, the traditional form of town-meeting government could not possibly deal with the complicated and often highly technical problems that suburban communities face today. Even so, one sometimes has an uneasy feeling, glancing at the clock on the wall, that the system is being strained to the limit. The laudable tradition of the United States Congress, by which freshmen members hold their peace during their period of initiation, does not always hold true here.* Then there are the compulsive speakers who may find their role personally therapeutic, but who seldom throw light on the matter at hand. A single such individual, ignoring the groans that are occasioned by his rising to his feet, can bring the machinery almost to a halt, apparently unaware that if many others pre-empted the amount of time he did, town-meeting government itself would become impossible.

Leaving aside these aberrations, there may be other more serious errors in judgment. The one I remember best occurred not at the official town meeting, but at the candidates' night held by the League of Women Voters the week before. A group of cronies had gotten together to present themselves as a "slate" of candidates for several of the principal town offices, including Moderator, Selectman, and Member of the Planning Board. Alas for their hopes, they did not understand the town they were ostensibly so eager to serve. The candidate for Moderator, waving aloft a letter supporting his opponent, implied that the signers could expect future favors if their man got in; the aspirant for Planning Board baldly accused his rival of seeking the office for personal gain. For the first time in memory, boos filled the hall. The attempted take-over was never repeated. One recalls a comment in Lockridge's study of Dedham: "No man, group of men, or single institution could run away with the town, and generally none wanted to try."

In speaking to an article before town meeting, a sense of humor may be an asset, but heavy irony can backfire. I think of the evening when the major land purchase in Lincoln's open space program came up for decision. The sum

* It did hold true for Lincoln's historian, Charles Francis Adams, who, when he moved from Quincy to Lincoln, was no novice at town meetings. He felt at home at once. Nevertheless, "a new-comer, I naturally took no part."

was large and the debate was long. A two-thirds vote was needed for passage. For a while, the issue seemed in doubt. Assurance of success came at last when a speaker in opposition made sour and sarcastic references to skunks and woodchucks and bluebirds and the like as the only beneficiaries of such parkland. Each reference to an animal was greeted with applause, which the speaker mistakenly believed was directed toward him, whereas it was in fact for the skunks and woodchucks and bluebirds. As he resumed his seat with satisfaction, there were no further doubts that the motion would pass.

It is a rare meeting that does not have its light moments. Sometimes these are set pieces, like the learned debate, replete with apt quotation and well-prepared spontaneity, that took place each year between two descendants of a leading Revolutionary family on the subject of Fourth of July fireworks. More often the humor is inadvertent. Who can forget the meeting in the old town hall at which new water pipes were requested by residents of North Lincoln to replace those that had grown rusty with age? "Look here," cried an indignant lady, rising to her feet and holding aloft a glass jar of tea-colored liquid. "Here is a sample of my water!"

Town meetings are serious but they are seldom solemn. Apparently from earliest times, they have been marked by a lack of pretense, by "an absolute, almost rude political equality" based not so much on law as on custom. Though the town officers and committee members sit up front for convenience in speaking, they are in every sense on the same level as the rest; the structure of the meeting is one of order without hierarchy. Tough questions to the committees, which often precede general discussion, are fielded with competence, and foolish ones with good grace. At times the ship of state seems firmly aground, not in most cases on a major reef but on some minor mudbank that invites turgid orations unhampered by the need for substance. Yet somehow, while the clock hands inexorably turn and softly clacking needles knit sweaters by the yard,* the business of the town gets done. Seldom does one hear those welcome words, "The meeting is adjourned" without feeling that, despite all the tedium and irrelevancies, wisdom has at length prevailed. Those whose pet measures have failed to pass may be disappointed but rarely bitter, since they have had every chance to be heard, and will have many chances more.

Haltingly, often inefficiently, the system nevertheless works — as it has for over three hundred years. It is old yet it is far from obsolete. As John Gardner wrote recently of Common Cause, "Individuals have to gain some sense of being able to act in relation to the group, be heard, have their say, belong."

---

* A recent town meeting was pleasantly interrupted while a vagrant ball of wool, which had rolled down the gently sloping floor to the front of the auditorium, was passed back hand to hand under ten rows of seats to its embarrassed owner.

CHAPTER 12

"It is no slight thing to be of a New England town."
— Senator George Frisbie Hoar, at the dedication of the Lincoln
   Library

Midpassage

To appreciate the elasticity and the durability of New England town government, one has only to glance back a hundred years to a time when Lincoln was in midpassage between the birth of the nation and the celebration of its bicentennial in 1975. In 1875 the Town Report, which had only recently begun to appear in printed form, ran to twenty pages, with reports by the Treasurer, the Selectmen, and the School Committee. By 1975 it had grown more than tenfold. The town's business required the service of eighteen elected officers and committees and over eighty other officials or boards appointed by these officers, ranging from the ancient and now honorary position of Fence Viewer to commissions dealing with such modern problems as land conservation and the control of aircraft noise. A century ago, the physical appearance of the landscape and the daily life of the people were both governed by the fact that Lincoln was an almost purely agricultural community. A muster roll of those liable for military service during the Civil War lists forty-four farmers and only one each of seven other occupations: clerk, market man, miller, merchant, fruit dealer, medical student, and milkman. In these circumstances, the maintaining of "open space" was no problem. The need for a planning board, a conservation commission, a building code, was as yet inconceivable.

Today, by contrast, only four residents of Lincoln describe themselves as "farmer," and three of these are over sixty years of age. Wholly different forces are shaping the land and the resultant way of life.

Does this indicate that the past is meaningless, that talk about preservation of the "rural values" is so much wasted breath? Or can we detect beneath the surface — like those Roman roads in Britain visible only from the air — certain enduring bonds with an earlier time: bonds strong and supple enough to have survived the relatively sudden metamorphosis from a self-contained body of Anglo-Saxon families making their living from the land to a sophisticated community of mixed origin and diverse professions, dwelling *on* the land but generally earning their bread elsewhere? Do these voices from long-forgotten town meetings, these earnest accountings by town fathers long dead, still have a familiar ring?

To a Lincoln resident of a century ago, these would have been idle questions. In 1875, over a third of those living in the town had been born there and the words recorded in the town books were the words of their ancestors. The main business of the town was much as it had been from the beginning: upkeep and extension of the roads, housing and staffing of the schools, collection of taxes, expansion of the cemetery, repairs on the town hall. Only one item, dominant in early days, was now missing: support of the minister and the meetinghouse. Church and state had officially separated in 1830, and a decade later there were two parishes, Congregational and Unitarian, each supported by its own congregation. No longer did the whole town gather together on the Sabbath, for long hours of worship and gossip at the "nooning." A social as well as a religious bond had been broken.

Two outward and visible signs of these inward and spiritual events had for many years graced the slopes of Lincoln

Hill. One was the "white church," built by the Unitarians when they established their own parish. The other was Lincoln's first town hall. From time immemorial, town meetings and religious services had both been held in the meetinghouse, here as elsewhere in New England. When separation came and the meetinghouse was no longer town property, the need for a new building to accommodate both town meetings and public events became acute. For some years, the citizens had made do with the Center School. Finally in the spring of 1848 a building committee had presented "a skeleton of a plan" for a modest, two-story, neoclassical building to cost about $1500. Despite difficulty in raising the money, the project had been approved and the carpenters had been swift, for by December the voters held the first town meeting in their new home opposite the old meetinghouse. The purposes to which it was to be put are spelled out in the town records; they show a public concern for issues broader than the business of local government. "The Town Hall shall be opened without charge for all Political, Temperance, Antislavery and Peace meetings and Lecturers, for Lyceum and Singing Schools, for Picnicks, Fairs and Sabbath School celebrations and for all Literary and Scientific lectures to which no admission fee is charged." Lincoln's first high school was established in the ground floor room. But when it was proposed that the new town hall might be hired for dancing schools and parties, there was a long and bitter debate; the Puritan tradition was not yet dead. At length the motion passed "after much talk and excited feeling on the subject."

The town hall was a source of civic pride; it symbolized the concern and active participation in town affairs which remain today our most important legacy from the past. Yet it is comforting to note that, then as now, this concern required an occasional nudge. In the case of special town meetings, a constable was sent around to each house six days in advance to assure full attendance. And though the number of articles to be debated may look small to us, there was apparently the same old problem of voters slipping away before the meeting was over. When the vital question of building the town hall was under consideration, this article was taken up first for action "whilst there was still a full house." And well that it was, since it passed by the narrow margin of 45 to 42. Probably never before or since have three votes made such a difference in the life — and in the appearance — of the town.

Change would come very slowly to Lincoln Hill over the ensuing years. In the 1870s it must have looked much as it did in the 1840s: the houses well apart, with wide open spaces on either side of the gravel road, the Common below the town hall dominated by the chestnut tree that appears on the town seal. From the slope beyond rose the weathered headstones of early Lincoln settlers. Looking out from the hill, the eye would travel far over rolling fields and orchards, unobstructed by the forest which the farmer still kept at bay.

Though the outward appearance of Lincoln was, no doubt, much as it always had been, a startling change was taking place beneath the surface. New blood from overseas was pouring into an old and dominantly Anglo-Saxon community. By the early eighties, the Lincoln School Committee was struggling with the problem of teaching pupils "belonging to four nationalities, differing widely in their ages and attainments." Town birth records for the previous decade show children of foreign-born parents outnumbering those of native Americans by more than two to one. The vast majority of these were Irish, with scatterings from England, from various European countries, and from nearby Nova Scotia (which later ranked second only to Ireland). Lincoln was within the orbit of Boston; and in the half-century following the Great Famine, the Irish had become a dominant element of the Boston population.

Some of the newcomers became independent farmers. A number of them, to judge from annual payrolls, earned at least part of their living by working for the town. Later on many of them were employed on the large estates, as farmers and farm managers, a few as coachmen and chauffeurs. Some became substantial landowners and took an active part in town affairs. Up to the turn of the century, however, most town offices remained in the hands of the old families, some of whom had held the reins since the days of the Puritans.

In 1875 Lincoln still had only about 800 residents on over 9000 acres. Most of the 47 properties listed in the tax rolls as "farms" comprised from fifty to a hundred acres or more, though many families with smaller holdings owned a barn, a cow or two, and perhaps a few pigs. Dairying was an important source of income; few really large herds, but a total of as many cows and calves as people. Draft horses had largely replaced oxen for farm work, even though (in the words of Dr. Stearns's grandson) "oxen were considered more hardy than horses, more powerful and less expensive. On most farms the ground was so rocky that the slower pace of oxen, while plowing, saved many a dig in the ribs and broken plow." Yet in 1875 there were only a few yokes of oxen left.

Such local industry as had flourished in earlier times was now all but dead. The tannery, the brickyard, the woolen mill were gone. There were still two cider mills, a grist-mill, a few sawmills, an icehouse, two shops and — heralding a new type of farming — a pickle factory.

High society was conspicuously absent. Only one family in five owned a carriage (as opposed to a farm wagon) and there were few places that could be called country estates. The outstanding one was "The Grange" or Codman Farm, the old estate of Lincoln's principal founder, Chambers Russell, which in 1800 had been described by the Governor's wife as "the handsomest place in America." Developed by John Codman as a country seat in the English style, it was still an impressive establishment, presided over by the "Mansion House," a Bulfinch building of the Federalist period which remains a Lincoln landmark.

If Lincoln had few conspicuously rich, it also had few conspicuously poor. Generally there were only three or four paupers or insane. In 1875, the former were "cared for

by Mr. Jones for the sum of $800." When necessary, residents certified as insane were sent to a "lunatic hospital" at
the town's expense, but not until the overseers of the poor
had tried their best to place the burden elsewhere. As for
so-called "tramps," the sums expended on them suggest that
they were given minimum assistance and maximum encouragement to move on. Year in and year out, the cost of
poor relief averaged only about $1000.

A century ago, as in colonial times, the maintenance of
"highways and bridges" was a major expense, running to a
third or more of the annual budget. By modern standards
these dirt roads were scarcely "highways." They were
muddy and frost-heaved in the spring, blanketed with dust
in summer, snow-covered in winter ("Voted to have a set
of Runners procured for the Hearse."). But in terms of
sweat and hard cash they represented an immense effort —
and for poorer residents a chance for financial relief. The
town was divided into districts and each Highway Surveyor
was instructed to "notify each tax payer in his district when
he will work on the Road, and give each a chance to work
out his taxes" at the rate of two dollars a day for a man and
team. In the circumstances, new road-building within the
town was not lightly undertaken; witness the vote "to
choose a committee to oppose the laying out of the Road
[Dr. Russell's] with all their might." Payments for blasting rock, for powder and fuse, for "lumber for bridge and
posts," for hundreds of hours of manual labor, give an idea
of roadwork before the days of the bulldozer. The perennial headache was the repair of the two county roads.
North Great Road (the historic battle road) was in early
times the main thoroughfare from Boston to northwestern
New England. Here passed the four-horse mail stage, with
BOSTON, KEENE, BRATTLEBORO, and U.S.M. inscribed
in large letters on its side. According to a member of the
family, the Brooks Tavern, where the road went by "Brooks

Village," enjoyed "the largest patronage of any hostelry out of Boston." At nearly all hours of the day, one might see "large teams of six and eight horses, innumerable wagons and carriages. In the winter a score or more two-horse pungs from Vermont or New Hampshire often made the journey together." Again and again the town Treasurer had to borrow thousands of dollars to keep this and the South County Road in repair, as required by the county commissioners. The town cast around for some better way to handle the problem, but got nowhere. "After much talk and the rejection of several motions," wrote the Clerk with an almost audible sigh of resignation, "it was moved to repair the Roads and Bridges in the same manner as last year." Surveyor of Highways was not a popular job; more than one man turned it down, and the Assessors, when officially asked to double as Surveyors, wisely refused.

By 1875 the Selectmen, in wrestling with highway problems, were already thinking in modern terms, not simply of the necessities of travel but more particularly of real estate values. Good roads, they pointed out, enhance the value of property in the town. Residents still worked out their taxes by hard labor on the town highways and bridges, but the pace of life was making this increasingly difficult. "When the farmers of the town kept strong teams of oxen," wrote the Selectmen, "and carried on farming in such a manner as left them a space of leisure time in the spring, soon after the ground thawed out, the farmers by dividing the town into districts could repair the roads; but now, when the farmer to be successful must arrange his work so as to have no leisure time for his team or help, some other provision must be made." Why was there no longer free time when the ground had thawed but was not yet ready for sowing? What had happened to put the farmers of Lincoln and nearby towns under such pressure?

The scattering of Irish names on the 1875 labor rolls suggests the answer. Thirty years earlier, the Fitchburg Railroad, built by Irish immigrants, had begun to operate from Boston as far west as Concord. It was the most momentous event in Lincoln's history since the battle of April 19, 1775.

At Walden Pond, Henry Thoreau heard "the iron horse make the hills echo with his snort like thunder, shaking the earth with his feet, and breathing fire and smoke from his nostrils." He was well aware that the locomotive whistle was screaming a message from the city merchants that no farmer could ignore. "Nor is any man so independent on his farm that he can say them nay." As mentioned previously, the coming of the railroads, together with the opening of the Erie Canal, was to change the face of New England. Wheat from the West began to flood the eastern markets. Sheep pastures, cleared from the forest by incredible toil of men and oxen, rock farms with their thin skin of soil, could not compete with the natural grasslands and the rich black earth of the Midwest. Already by midcentury deserted farmhouses were conspicuous in the landscape; pasture and cropland were returning to woods. Great stone walls, as wide as an oxcart — forgotten cellar holes, with lilac bushes at the corners — these would soon be the only momentoes of a vanished era. Young men left the family farm to work in the factories that were harnessing the waterpower along the "fall line." With its manufactures and its shipping, its mammoth red brick mills and fast graceful clippers, southern New England was entering a period of economic prosperity. But not for the farmer; and Lincoln was a farming town. Even had the residents wished it, Lincoln had neither the location, the waterpower, nor the natural resources to become an industrial community. And so with the advent of the railroad, bringing cheap farm products from the West and cordwood from the limitless forests of Maine, it must have seemed only a matter of time before the thrifty Lincoln farmer could no longer make a living — before a traditional way of life would vanish once and for all.

That it did not vanish, that the farmers of Lincoln did not all go bankrupt, speaks well for Yankee resourcefulness. Since the full impact of the railroad was not felt for some years, there was time to adjust to new conditions and to exploit new opportunities. Boston was growing populous and rich, offering a ready outlet both for dairy products and for the perishable fruits and vegetables of local truck farms. And by providing quick year-round transportation to the city, the railroad made possible a new kind of farming that would prove to be Lincoln's salvation. With an eye to the Boston market, progressive Lincoln farmers began raising crops under glass.

Grown out of season, strawberries, lettuce, asparagus, cucumbers, and such luxuries commanded top prices in Boston. Indeed it is said that a greenhouse in Lincoln would pay for itself in a single year. Not only vegetables but cut flowers were in constant demand. One of Lincoln's older residents recalls from his childhood the sweet heavy odor of a greenhouse bright with violets, as he watched the young farmhands wrap them in bundles to catch the early morning train to town.

Later on came a less fragrant crop: pigs. Though "swine" had been conspicuously on the scene in New England since the beginning, one associates large-scale hog-raising with the Midwest corn belt. Yet not long ago there were more pigs per acre in Middlesex County, Massachusetts, than in any other county in the United States. My wife and I had this surprising statistic brought forcibly to our attention when we moved to Lincoln from Cambridge forty-odd years ago. The field just across the road from our sleeping porch was regularly fertilized with pig manure, an occasional dead piglet being thrown in for good measure. The stench assured us that we were indeed in the country. Moreover we could take comfort in the fact that the country and the city had, when it came to pigs, a perfect symbiotic relationship. Lincoln hogs, fed on Boston garbage, would eventually return to the city as pork and bacon, leaving the Lincoln fields richer for their presence. Recycling at its best.

So by one means or another, rural Lincoln survived the competition brought to bear by the iron horse. In 1875 it was still a self-supporting country town, with few if any residents earning their living in Boston. Its concerns were, with occasional exceptions, purely local. One major exception was of course the Civil War, only a decade in the past. Yet even this holocaust did not deeply affect the small Massachusetts towns. Immediately after the firing on Fort Sumter there was a short burst of enlistment. "Three Lincoln men went in Captain Prescott's company in April 1861," recalled Dr. Edward W. Emerson, "four in Captain Barrett's." (How those Revolutionary names persist!) Five more were later provided by the town for three years' service. The town meeting voted to pay ten dollars a month to men who volunteered, together with any equipment not provided by the state. A committee was also appointed "to carry round a paper and see who they can get to enlist as a home guard." These home guard recruits were obviously Lincoln residents. But as in Revolutionary days, the town apparently hired men wherever it could get them to fulfill its draft quota for the Union army. "Nine months men" could be had for $200 apiece; there is nothing in the record to suggest that they were necessarily citizens of Lincoln.

Some Lincoln men, however, did die in the conflict. The town paid for bringing home and burying in the town cemetery the bodies of those who fell. Four years after Appomattox, it was proposed at town meeting that a tablet or monument be erected honoring all Lincolnians who served in the war. When we look at the Civil War monuments that dominate many a New England town common, we may be thankful that the committee eventually settled on marble gravestones for the dead — four in all. By the time they were erected, the town had returned to business as usual.

A perennial budget item was the upkeep of the town cemeteries. This is the one area in which the town seemed most self-conscious about appearances. In the Selectmen's

Report for 1875, it ranks second in importance only to the repair of highways and bridges. "We could call the attention of the town to the condition of the cemeteries. We have three, each of them small in extent, and so crowded in some parts, and the lots of some families are well cared for, while other lots are sadly neglected, chiefly for the reason that it is nobody's business to have charge of it. If the town should choose a committee each year to have charge of the cemeteries, we feel sure they would be improved in appearance. There is a sum of money now in the hands of the ladies of the town, raised by a fair and tea party, which they desire to expend in the manner indicated when they can obtain the aid and advice of some one who has authority in the matter."

Agitation for improvement of the burying grounds had been going on for decades. In gradiloquent terms, fortified by Biblical reference and pious verse, an earlier committee had appealed to the town to keep up with the Joneses. "The taste for improving and adorning cemeteries is everywhere spreading . . . other towns are doing much in the matter, and unless we would be left behind in the march of civilization and race for improvement we must take care of our burying grounds." After citing precedents going back to Abraham, the author of the report concludes that, if the recommendations are accepted, "in a few years our grave yards instead of being eyesores and plague spots on the fair face of creation overrun with bushes and briers inhabited by foxes and woodchucks would become 'a garden of graves and paradise of God, where forests wave and flowers bloom.' " The town thereupon appropriated one hundred dollars for the purpose. Apparently this was not sufficient, since fifteen years later the committee was still pleading that the "gloom and horror" of the old burying ground be transformed into "a scene of sylvan beauty."

On a spring day in 1850 Henry Thoreau had visited "a retired, now almost unused, graveyard in Lincoln." This was the old burying ground near the Flints, where the first townsmen, and later the five British grenadiers who fell on April 19, 1775, had been interred. Thoreau would not, I think, have objected to the foxes and the woodchucks. "I am not offended by the odor of the skunk in passing sacred places. I am invigorated rather. It is a reminiscence of immortality borne on the gale." Near the as yet unmarked grave of the British soldiers he read the epitaph of the Negro slave Sippio Brister that inspired the familiar passage in *Walden*. "He is styled . . . 'a man of color' as if he were discolored. It also told me, with staring emphasis, when he died; which is but an indirect way of informing me that he ever lived. With him dwelt Fenda, his hospitable wife, who told fortunes, yet pleasantly, — large, round, and black, blacker than any of the children of night, such a dusky orb as never rose on Concord before or since."

The old cemetery was eventually restored, no doubt owning to the addition of ten ladies to the committee — one of the early appearances of women on town boards. Today as one reads the inscriptions on the headstones of the three Lincoln burying grounds, one is reminded of how uncertain life was only a few generations ago. Many lived to a ripe old age, but consumption was the great killer of the young. Dr. Stearns's grandson, for example, had two brothers and a sister; all died of consumption before they reached twenty-one. Ralph Waldo Emerson, before he moved to Concord, had lost his first wife and two brothers from the same affliction; a few years later it would take his beloved first son.

It was in the cultural life of Lincoln, as distinguished from the routine of town government, that the ladies came into their own: in the schools and, from the seventies on, in the public library. In 1875, all four primary schools — North, East, Center, and South — and the high school were staffed by women. Each primary school had three terms — summer, fall, and winter — and each had about thirty scholars. Attendance was a constant problem, and so was the turnover of teachers. This year the South School had three teachers in succession; and the teacher of the East School left for a better job elsewhere, to be succeeded by her sister whose "systematic methods," reports the School Committee, "are quite like her sister's, so that the change in teachers has produced hardly the slightest difference in . . . the manner of conducting classes." The method of teaching is summarized elsewhere in the report in terms that embody the essence of the "little red schoolhouse": "clock-like movement, systematic and patient drill, thorough study, stereotyped methods whose value is all the more proved, because they stand the test of time." A few years later a young teacher, trained in more progressive methods, was forced out of her job, despite the backing of the School Committee, by a minority group of reactionary parents.

Things were different at the high school. But even here there was but a single teacher for thirty pupils and a variety of subjects, while the changing composition of the student body from term to term made any sustained course of study impossible. "As heretofore," reports the Committee, "the large number of studies has taxed the ingenuity of the teacher to undue . . . division of her time." She did her best by specializing in "bookkeeping, mathematics and elocution in the Winter Term, when the school has its largest attendance of boys and young men; and French, Botany, History, etc., in the Summer Term, when the attendance of young ladies is relatively larger." And somehow she survived to see the year through.

But as a rule the high school teachers were young men recently out of college, some of whom lightened the academic routine by capitalizing on Lincoln's rural setting. Of one it is reported: "His long walks, and talks with his scholars while roaming the fields and woods, seeking specimens, greatly endeared him to them." Though no one could match the teaching record of Dr. Charles Stearns a century earlier, the standards he set had been kept up — as witness the comment by the famous preacher and social reformer, Theodore Parker, to an audience in his native town of Lexington: "The little town on the hill yonder has long maintained so high a standard that Lexington has depended on her for many of its teachers." One suspects that higher salaries paid by larger towns like Lexington may explain the high turnover of Lincoln schoolteachers.

An occasional Lincoln boy was accepted by Harvard, to the great pride of the School Committee and the town. "The fact that a boy trained in our High School — with no other appliances of learning than is found in the home of the average New England farmer — performing all the while a large amount of manual labor — was able to enter Harvard University *without conditions*, speaks volumes in praise of the school and the teachers."

Women had been voluntarily added to the Cemetery Committee; now by state law they were given the right to vote for members of the School Committee — whose chairman at the time happened to be the same master of purple prose who had once sought to make the Lincoln cemetery a "paradise of God." Recognizing that the new law might be an entering wedge for woman suffrage, "hitherto a subject of jest or scepticism," he magnanimously concedes that it could lead to peace, prosperity, and progress rather than to misguidance and disaster. Queen Victoria, he reminds us, had cleared the English Court of scandal. "If the influence of women shall be brought to bear more largely or directly upon State or National affairs, we see no reason for supposing the people will be less wise or virtuous, or the Nation less prosperous and happy." On the contrary, it might lead to greater moral purity in high places and hasten "the time when the kingdoms of this earth shall become the kingdoms of our Lord and his Christ . . ."

While awaiting the coming of the millennium, the School Committee addressed itself to such mundane matters as an outbreak of whooping cough, homesickness on the part of a young lady teacher, lack of discipline in the classroom, and chronically poor attendance. The committee had protested in vain against "the unwisdom of scholars deserting the schools for baseball contests, musters and cattle-shows" or taking part in athletic competitions when health and strength could be as well developed "by swinging the axe or scythe, or guiding the plow, as by handling the bat or oar." The town fathers were proud to be living in a rural community. More than one eminent citizen of Boston, they liked to recall, had in his boyhood been sent from the city to develop muscle and character on Lincoln farms.

In 1875 New England was still fresh from the cultural revolution that had begun in Boston early in the century and reached its peak in Lincoln's mother town of Concord. Ralph Waldo Emerson and Bronson Alcott were still alive; Henry Thoreau and Nathaniel Hawthorne only recently dead. Books that would become classics were finding a new generation of readers; literary magazines and lyceums were flourishing. The farmers of Lincoln had not lagged behind in this universal drive for intellectual self-improvement. As early as 1832 a group of them had met in the old center schoolhouse to found the Lincoln Lyceum, for "our own improvement in Knowledge, the advance of Popular Education and the diffusion of useful information throughout the community generally . . ." Once a week they would meet at the center school to hear a lecture and to debate some previously chosen question, such as "Is the Mechanic more beneficial to the community than the Farmer?" (Decided in favor of the farmer.) The Puritan heritage was still strong. Morals, they decided, were more important than intellect; knowledge conveyed more power than wealth, novel reading was a waste of time. In January of 1847 they argued over the justice of the war with Mexico. The following year, at a time when Concord was deeply involved in the "underground railway," they wrestled with the moral dilemma: was it justifiable to assist a fugitive slave to escape? Not all discussions were so solemn, however. Whether out of gallantry or humility (since the disputants, though not the audience, were all men) they decided that the female character had greater influence on society than the male; but they apparently gave up on such questions as "Ought early marriage to be encouraged?" or "Ought a young man in choosing a wife to look out for beauty or for wealth?"

The lectures — ranging in subject from Socrates to the rights of women, from popery to punctuality, from electromagnetism to the love of nature — drew largely upon nearby talent. Henry Thoreau's brilliant young friend Charles Stearns Wheeler spoke on ornithology. Thoreau himself delivered at least three lectures, the first on January 19, 1847.* The second — on March 6, 1849 — gave the farmers of Lincoln the rare opportunity of being present at the creation of a classic. "They then listened to a lecture from Mr. Thoreau of Concord, taken from his journal of a life in the woods." Five years later, they could read in *Walden* the words they had heard that night. Thoreau's third lecture, on "His Travels in Canada," would eventually be published in *A Yankee in Canada*.

Ralph Waldo Emerson also spoke no less than three times in Lincoln: on "Oratory and Eloquence," on "Beauty," and on "Individual Life." The Lyceum lectures lasted at least until 1856, though the debates had been abandoned somewhat earlier.

Emerson wrote in his journal: "Remember that a scholar wishes that every book, chart, and plate belonging to him should draw interest every moment by circulation." Yet in 1875 Lincoln, for all its interest in schools and in self-improvement, did not yet have a proper public library. Back in 1798 her famous pastor and schoolteacher, the Reverend Charles Stearns, had joined with some thirty other prominent citizens, including Eleazer Brooks, to form the Lincoln Social Library Society, "for the encouragement and promotion of literature and useful information" — each member contributing two dollars to get it started. Twice it dissolved

---

* The subject of the lecture is not recorded, but one may speculate. Immediately following it, the Lyceum chose as a topic for debate: "Is it expedient to obey *all laws* whether just or unjust?" The previous summer Thoreau had spent a night in jail for refusing to pay his poll tax in protest against our government's policies; in January of 1848 he explained his action in a Concord lecture on "the relation of the individual to the state," later to be known by the familiar title of *Civil Disobedience*.

and reorganized with new membership. The records end in 1848, but it is characteristic of Lincoln that, when a town library was finally built, four of the five trusteees were descendants of Stearns and his group.

The seed for the present library was planted in 1870 when the widow* of a distinguished and wealthy Harvard professor from Lincoln gave his collection of a thousand volumes to the town. These were augmented from other sources, including "books that remained from the old Social Library, Agricultural and District School Libraries" and gifts from private citizens. By good fortune, the town was then building a new schoolhouse at the center, freeing for library purposes the room formerly used by the high school. The Committee promptly set about to make it both useful and comfortable, with tables and lamps, curtains on the windows and "means of warming" — suggesting that former schoolroom conditions may have been somewhat Spartan. The 1875 annual town meeting passed a vote of thanks to two ladies for arranging the books and "preparing the room and furnishing it in such good taste as to make it at once an honor and ornament to the town."

The townspeople must have been thirsty for reading matter, since 700 volumes were taken out in the six months following the opening. Slowly the collection grew until, in 1884, when it had reached 3000 volumes, a grandson of a founder of the old Library Society gave it a splendid house of its own. Architecturally, the new building was of the period, "reminding one," wrote the eloquent chairman of the School Committee, "of those ancient cloisters which were the home and fortresses of learning through ages of barbarism and progress."

No one was suggesting, of course, that Lincoln a hundred

* Mrs. John [Eliza] Farrar, described by Perry Miller as "a dedicated patroness of 'genius,' and a hostess in as grand a manner as Cambridge could then afford." It was probably Mrs. Farrar who introduced Emerson to Margaret Fuller in 1835.

years ago was a fortress of learning in the wilderness. But as part of the Concord region, linked with Boston by the railroad, it had been close to the center of intellectual ferment and commercial progress. Boston's material prosperity was indirectly responsible for the Lincoln Library; the donor obviously had not made his money on a farm. In this sense the resident of Lincoln was better situated than the "average New England farmer" referred to earlier by the School Committee. Yet his situation would have been of little moment had it not been for the devotion to the community that Joseph Brooks had expressed so long ago when he donated a bell to the first meetinghouse "for the love and regard that I have to the inhabitants of said Town."

Unlike neighboring Concord, the village on the hill remained virtually unknown. Yet it represented, as much as Concord itself, a harmony of man and his environment such as had inspired the great Concord writers to leave the uncongenial atmosphere of the city and seek truth in nature. One cannot write of Lincoln's past without recognizing the

cultural revolution that took place on her borders. Had
Thoreau been permitted by the owner of Flint's Pond to
build his cabin on its shores instead of at Walden across the
line in Concord, he would have found a different title for
his book, and Lincoln's place in literary history would have
been secure. Be that as it may, the inspiration that Emerson, Hawthorne, Alcott, Margaret Fuller, and, above all,
Thoreau found in the woods and fields around Concord is a
part of the Lincoln tradition, and an essential element in
any picture of man's relation to the land.

CHAPTER 13 ⌐

"Henry [Thoreau] talks about nature just as if she's been born and brought up in Concord."
— Mrs. Samuel Hoar

Man and Nature
in Concord

In the autumn of 1834, Ralph Waldo Emerson, age thirty-one and born in Boston, came to live at the Old Manse on the banks of the Concord River. No salute of guns or roll of drums greeted his arrival. Yet in retrospect it was an event as significant in its own way as the battle at the bridge a few steps downstream, which his patriot grandfather, the Reverend William Emerson, had witnessed that April morning almost six decades ago. Publication of Emerson's *Essay on Nature* two years after his arrival in Concord has been compared in the history of American literary culture to the events of 1775 in our political history. Emerson had begun his own war of independence: of freedom from literary bondage to Europe, of self-reliance — which in fact meant cultivation of one's own genius, relying on the presence of God in every man. "Hail to the quiet fields of my fathers!" he wrote in his Journal. "Henceforth I design not to utter any speech, poem or book that is not entirely and peculiarly my work."

To hold to such a lofty standard, Emerson relied throughout his life on one never-failing source of strength and inspiration: the world of nature. It was not the wild nature that early naturalist-explorers like André Michaux and William Bartram had found in the rugged Appalachians and the trackless swamps of Florida, that John James Au-

dubon was at this moment experiencing in the American
primeval forests and on the windswept coasts of Labrador,
that John Muir was later to find amid the glaciers of
Alaska. Nor, as picturesque scenery, could the valley of the
sluggish Musketaquid, the cliffs of Fairhaven Hill, the distant view of Wachusett and Monadnock be compared to the
mellow grandeur of England's Lake Country, which had
inspired the native poetry of William Wordsworth. Yet
this quiet Concord region — of which the town of Lincoln
is a part — nurtured the genius of Emerson and Thoreau,
of Hawthorne, of the Alcott family, until it came to rival
Boston as the literary capital of America. In every case the
fact that the writer was living close to the land, in a quiet
village apart from — though within reach of — the turmoil
of the city, shaped the style and substance of his work. In
no two cases, however, was the psychological reaction to
nature the same.

From his earliest days Emerson was vexed by what he
felt to be his awkwardness in company, his apparent coldness, his "lack of skill to live with men." He craved solitude — or so he thought — but was troubled by this yearning to escape. "Would it not be cowardly to flee out of
society and live in the woods?" he mused while visiting,
appropriately enough, the treeless city of Venice. Fortunately for American literature, he soon decided that it
would not. If society seemed obnoxious, nature was the
antidote; a man comes out of the wrangle of the shop and
the office, and sees the sky and the woods, and is a man
again.

Emerson's move to Concord came at a time of intellectual
and spiritual awakening: the half century from 1815 to
1865 that Van Wyck Brooks has called "the flowering of
New England." More and more young men in Boston and
elsewhere were revolting against the complacent, prosperous, materialistic society of urban America. A passion for

learning went along with a new social awareness. Schools were being revolutionized, religious doctrines were being questioned, lyceums were drawing crowds from all classes to share the latest ideas on philosophy, literature, science. Restless students were dropping out of college to seek truth in their own fashion. Dr. William Ellery Channing, Boston's saintly preacher, shared with his friends Wordsworth and Coleridge a mystical sense of the divinity of nature; his nephew and namesake, who would become Henry Thoreau's closest companion, left Harvard to live in a log cabin on the prairie before settling down in Concord. Thoreau's school friend and college roommate, Charles Stearns Wheeler (grandson of Dr. Charles Stearns, Lincoln's beloved pastor and romantic poet), built himself a hut on the shores of Flint's Pond in Lincoln while still an undergraduate; there Thoreau joined him for six weeks during a summer vacation and so got the idea for the later experiment at Walden.*

Much of this protest has a familiar ring. The doctrine that came to be known as transcendentalism sought truth through immediate preception, transcending the learning process; one cannot help thinking of Zen. Utopian communes like Brook Farm and Fruitlands glorified rural living, vegetarianism, and contact with the soil. Long hair, bright blouses, proclaimed freedom from convention; if there were fewer guitars, there were flutes. The very words echo across more than a century. "I want my place, my own place, my true place in the world," wrote Nathaniel Hawthorne, "my proper sphere, my thing . . ."

---

* Thoreau originally intended to build his cabin on the shores of Flint's Pond, but the owner refused permission. Thoreau took his revenge in the famous diatribe in *Walden*. "*Flint's Pond!*. . . What right has the unclean and stupid farmer, whose farm abutted on this sky water, whose shores he has ruthlessly laid bare, to give his name to it? Some skin-flint, who loved better the reflecting surface of a dollar, or a bright cent, in which he could see his own brazen face . . . who would carry the landscape, who would carry his God, to market, if he could get anything for him. . ."

Descendant of six generations of churchmen, himself a popular pastor and preacher while still in his twenties, Emerson nonetheless found that God was manifest in the wood as He was not in the sermon. He had reason to know, since shortly before coming to Concord he had sought in the solitude of the White Mountains an answer to the question that would determine the direction of his life: could he with complete honesty remain a minister in the Unitarian Church? The hour of decision had come when he realized that, in the light of his own convictions as well as his studies of church history, he could not accept the orthodox view of the holy communion. Was he, he wondered, being too conscientious, straining at gnats? "The most desperate scoundrels have been the over-refiners." Here among the mountains "the pinions of thought should be strong." They were. They gave him strength to break with a creed that he found effete and superannuated, to act on his belief that to be a good minister it may in some circumstances be necessary to leave the ministry. What made possible such a decision was his conviction that God is manifest throughout the universe. "The moral law lies at the centre of nature ... Every animal function from the sponge up to Hercules, shall hint or thunder to man the laws of right and wrong, and echo the Ten Commandments."

This was quite an assignment for the chickadees in the Concord woodlots and the ducks on the river. Despite his break with tradition, the blood of those Puritan divines still flowed in Emerson's veins. Reading *Nature* today, one is struck by the apparent contradiction between his exhilaration in the presence of wild nature and desire to live in harmony with it and, on the other hand, his acceptance of the Old Testament attitude that everything on earth has been put here exclusively for the use of man. He quotes with approval lines from the seventeenth-century psalmist George Herbert: "For us, the winds do blow,/the earth

doth rest, heaven move, and fountains flow." Nature, he
states flatly, is made to serve, to provide man with "raw
material which he may mould into what is useful." Yet
his intelligence — one might almost say his common sense
— will not quite allow him to swallow this doctrine whole,
even when the "use" is an intellectual one. "Have mountains, and waves, and skies, no significance but what we
consciously give them when we employ them as emblems
of our thoughts? . . . We are like travellers using the cinders
of a volcano to roast their eggs."

As a New England Puritan, Emerson may have been
compelled to seek a moral behind every facet of nature, but
as a poet and philosopher he relied on his spontaneous emotions. In the presence of nature a wild delight runs through
him: "I am glad to the brink of fear." On an April afternoon he and his friend Jones Very, the poet, are sitting on
the shores of Walden Pond, breathing the warm air and
watching fleets of ripples scudding across the water. For
once he seeks no moral, no lesson. "I said to my companion,
I declare this world is so beautiful that I can hardly believe
it exists."

Spontaneous response is one thing; deliberate pursuit of
the picturesque is quite another. Emerson scorned what he
termed "view-hunters." Though he admired, and in some
early poems echoed, William Wordsworth, he deplored the

way the latter tried consciously to distill poetry out of the
landscape, how "he mauls the moon and the waters and the
bulrushes, as his main business." Nature will always provide inspiration to her true lovers — common, everyday
scenes such as abounded in rural Concord. Climbing the
cliff above Fairhaven Bay with young Henry Thoreau,
watching the stars to the music of the hylas in the swamp,
he felt no hankering for vast landscapes, the sea, or Niagara. Concord would suffice.

*   *   *

It would suffice for Thoreau too, in a deeper sense than
Emerson ever knew. In all American literature there is no
writer so directly, so fiercely concerned, not simply with
the abstract concept of Nature, but with the living land itself. Emerson might have written happily, though differ-
ently, had he lived in a city; Thoreau never. The relationship between the two men, personal and literary, is unique.
Fourteen years the younger, inspired by reading Emerson's
Nature while still in his teens, Thoreau progressed rapidly
from the role of disciple to an unruly embodiment of the
older man's ideas. "Thoreau gives me, in flesh and blood
. . . my own ethics. His is far more real, in daily practically
obeying them, than I." In fact, Thoreau obeyed his own
instincts, which led him out of the study into the open, out
of tame country into wild, out of the comforting, man-
centered cosmos of his time into an unknown — and perhaps unknowable — universe.

Born in Concord in 1817, Henry David Thoreau came
naturally to his taste for the outdoors. In the words of a
family friend he "was not a superior scion on an inferior
stock; neither was he begotten by a northwest wind as
many have supposed." His father was poor but respectable,
his mother brainy and bustling, known as the most talka-
tive woman in town. Both liked to take the children to the

banks of the Assabet River, to Fairhaven Bay and Walden Pond, to Lee's Hill where, it is said, one of them narrowly escaped being born. With the help of scholarships, they put Henry through Harvard. In his commencement "part," he suggested, in defiance of the Puritan ethic, that "the world is more to be enjoyed than used." Back in Concord, living with his parents and an intimate of the Emerson household, he set about enjoying the world in his own way, sometimes with Emerson or their young poetical friend Ellery Channing, but best of all, alone. Afternoons were for walking, and it was a serious business. "It requires a direct dispensation from Heaven to become a walker . . . I spend four hours a day at least . . . sauntering through the woods and over the hills and fields, absolutely free from all worldly engagements." That word "sauntering" can be misleading. It is derived, Thoreau believed, from those people who roved the country in the Middle Ages, asking charity on the pretense that they were going to the Holy Land, *à la Sainte Terre:* they were *Sainte-Terrers*. For Thoreau, all land was holy. The earth, the river, the sky supplied the raw material in his search for truth. "I go out," he told Channing, "to see what I have caught in my traps which I set for facts."

Always he yearned for wildness, for "a nature which I cannot put my foot through." Relentless in his quest for knowledge, he had at the same time the mystic's need for the mysterious and unexplorable. "We need to witness our own limits transgressed, and some life pasturing freely where we never wander." In literature, he felt, tameness was synonymous with dullness.

In Thoreau's day, the Concord country could scarcely be called a wilderness, but one could still walk for miles without passing a house or crossing a road. And anyway, he rationalized in his journal, "It is vain to dream of a wilderness distant from ourselves . . . I shall never find in the wilds of Labrador any greater wildness than in some recess in Concord, i.e., than I import into it." So he was able to go round the world by the Old Marlborough Road, and to make an even longer journey at Walden Pond.

He took pride in finding his inspiration in the commonest events. He could hear "all of music" in the humming of a telegraph wire, and discover Nova Zembla in a frozen swamp. After he had been wading one day in a shallow mud-hole, he entered in his journal a superb description of a mud turtle capturing a hornpout, concluding with the comment: "I had no idea there was so much going on in Heywood's meadow." He would not, he boasted, accept "the proudest Paris" in exchange for his native village. Concord, he said, was his garden: larger and more attractive than any artificial garden he had ever read of. He took joy in the various miniature worlds of nature. "In a small brook like this,"* he writes on April 1, 1852, "there are many adjuncts to increase the variety which are wanting in a river or, if present, cannot be attended to; even dead leaves and twigs vary the ripplings and increase the foam. And the very lichens on the rocks of the run are an important ornament, which in the great waterfall are wont to be overlooked." As Henry Miller has written of him: "He found, by opening his eyes, that life provides everything necessary for man's peace and enjoyment."

Despite his disclaimers Thoreau would, I imagine, have gone farther afield had he been able to afford it; he made the most of what was within reach. He loved the rocky slopes of Mount Monadnock, the beaches of Cape Cod, the forests of Maine. The thought of the American West filled him with longing; romantically, he saw the backwoodsman living in paradise. Emerson complained that Henry wanted to go to Oregon, not London. One sometimes wishes that it

---

* Saw Mill Brook, in Lincoln, which flows from Sandy Pond into Mill Brook, and thence into Concord.

could have been he, instead of Emerson, who visited John
Muir among the redwoods a decade after Thoreau's death.
What a meeting that would have been! The styles of the
two writers are very different: Muir ecstatic, full of superla-
tives; Thoreau spare, laconic. Muir was an activist, fighting for conservation, founding the Sierra Club; Thoreau
was a solitary philosopher. But in their basic beliefs they
were brothers. "Only by going alone in silence, without
baggage," wrote Muir, "can one truly get into the heart of
the wilderness." Both despised the smug belief that the
world was made especially for man — a presumption, Muir
remarked, not supported by the facts. Their stance was not
one of misanthropy but of humility. They had too much
humor to put themselves at the center of the universe.

"I am naturally no hermit," Thoreau declared in *Walden*. "I think that I love society as much as most." However, his scorn of ostentation and cant drew him away
from the more prosperous and pious among his neighbors
toward the simple people: the farmers, the woodchoppers,
the hunters and the fishermen, the Irish laborers working
on the railroad, and above all to the young. "This youthful,
cheery figure was a familiar one in our house," wrote Edward W. Emerson, the philosopher's son. "When he, like
the Pied Piper of Hamelin, sounded his note in the hall, the
children must needs come and hug his knees, and he strug-
gled with them, nothing loath, to the fireplace, sat down
and told stories . . . of squirrels, muskrats, hawks he had
seen that day; the duel of mud-turtles in the river; the
Great Homeric battle of red and black ants." Contrast this
with Emerson's remark that he would as soon think of taking Thoreau's arm as taking the arm of an elm tree. Or with
Elizabeth Hoar's telling comment: "I love Henry, but I
don't like him." He could be prickly, notably when he felt
that he was being patronized. A clergyman visiting the
Thoreaus, after Henry had returned from Walden Pond,

clapped him on the shoulder: "So here's the chap who camped in the woods!" Thoreau turned around: "And here's the chap that camps in a pulpit."

He idealized the concept of Woman; actual women he kept at a distance. Despite all his observations of natural behavior in the wild, and his recognition of man as a part of nature, he was squeamish about sex. Sensuality had no place in his pure image of human love. He found his ecstasies elsewhere. It has been sagely remarked that Henry Thoreau could get more out of ten minutes with a woodchuck than most men could from a night with Cleopatra.

Throughout his life Thoreau was painfully aware of his apparent coldness toward his acquaintances, and seeks to explain it to himself: "It is not that I am too cold, but that our warmth and coldness are not of the same nature; hence when I am absolutely warmest, I may be coldest to you." Again he writes with resignation in his journal: "It appears to be a law that you cannot have a deep sympathy with both man and nature. Those qualities that bring you near to the one estrange you from the other."

This, I think, is one of Thoreau's least convincing generalizations — not true even when applied to himself. Ellery Channing, who perhaps knew him best, found "no whim of coldness" in him; rather he thought of his friend as a natural stoic. Winter was his favorite season: a landscape stripped bare, trees etched in sharp silhouette against the sky. How cheerful the chime of icicles as his oar grazed the button-bushes on the river in December! Now the sound of the woodchopper's ax, the distant clarion of the cock, come clear and bell-like through the frosty air. "The wonderful purity of nature at this season is a most pleasing fact," he writes of a winter walk. "A cold and searching wind drives away all contagion." Purity. Innocence. No false notes, no soft edges, no compromise. "Better a monosyllabic life than a ragged and muttered one; let its report be short and round like a rifle, so that it may hear its own echo in the surrounding silence."

Emerson, to whom a bird was a bird, wondered at Thoreau's knowledge of natural history. But Thoreau never called himself a scientist. Quite otherwise. This was in an era when, as he put it, science was studied as a dead language. He hated museums with their pickled, bloated specimens; amid these corpses he felt as if he were in a tomb. A century before his time, he was concerned with the living plant, the living animal. "A man's interest in a

single bluebird," he wrote to his friend Daniel Ricketson, "is worth more than a complete but dry list of the fauna and flora of a town." Yet he scorned "the mealy-mouthed enthusiasm of the mere lover of nature." As a botanist, he knew the Concord region so well that he claimed to be able to tell the date from what wildflowers were in bloom; his plant collection, now preserved at Harvard, is an invaluable source for modern scholars. While he was still in college a classmate (though finding him cold toward his fel-

lows) described him as "Nature's own child learning to
detect her wayside secrets. . . He saw more upon the ground
than anyone suspected to be there." A friend whose hobby
was the study of insects complained that young Thoreau
would have made a splendid entomologist if Emerson had
not spoiled him.

Thoreau's view of nature — and his own relation to it —
is, like his views on most subjects, replete with paradox. He
feels that it is important to consider the natural world from
a scientific point of view, yet equally important to ignore
existing knowledge and remain open to new impressions.
More than once he suggests that man cannot afford to look
at nature directly; that his response is dissipated by too
many observations — as indeed it is in the later volumes of
his own journal. A scrupulous recorder of detail, he is
nevertheless repelled by too many dry facts in the scientific literature. "Oh," he exclaims, "for a little Lethe."
Rationalizing, perhaps, his inability to identify certain
songbirds (in his early years he did not even own a spy-
glass) he delights in hearing them sing as freshly as if it
had been the first morning of creation. Always he seems
torn between a passion to see, to know, to understand and —
pulling him in the opposite direction — the fear that in
looking too closely the vision, the poetry, will be lost. By
his own admission, Thoreau was a mystic. The richest
function of nature, he believed, was to symbolize human
life, to become a fable or myth for man's inward experience. For him the value of a fact was that some day it
would flower into a truth: not by laborious deduction, but
by "direct intercourse and sympathy." Deeply read in
Oriental philosophy, he cherished his sudden moments of
illumination.

To put Thoreau in the category of "nature writer," as
was commonly done in his time, is therefore misleading.
As much as Emerson, he was a philosopher and conscious

literary artist. But whereas Emerson brought the woods to his study, Thoreau brought himself to the woods. Moralizing from nature came easily to Emerson; Thoreau increasingly saw it as a weakness. "What offends me most in my compositions is the moral element in them." Life and wildness were one; the world of nature existed for its own sake. A single hawk sailing through the upper air was worth a hundred hens. It is hard to imagine Emerson racing a fox through the snow, or feeling a sudden impulse to eat a woodchuck raw. Nor for all his pantheism would Emerson have written about a white pine: "It is as immortal as I am, and perchance will go to as high a heaven, there to tower above me still." James Russell Lowell, then editor of the *Atlantic Monthly*, was shocked by such blasphemy and cut the sentence out of Thoreau's article. Thoreau never wrote for him again.

Thoreau was a poet, and his great poem was his journal.* Here his daily observations, his speculations, his intuitions were ordered and refined, often crystallized to the point of aphorism: "How vain it is to sit down to write when you have not stood up to live!" "The best you can write will be the best you are." His love of paradox, which Emerson in the early days objected to as a literary trick, resulted at its best in the gnomic statements that sparkle through the Journal: "Such naked speech is the standing aside of words to make room for thoughts."

Thoreau's method of literary composition helped him to achieve this sense of immediacy. On his daily excursions he would pause occasionally to make brief, cryptic jottings in his homemade pocket notebook, perhaps on a hillside in early March, holding his paper tight against the wind. When he returned home, he expanded these notes in his

---

* "Is not the poet bound to write his own biography? Is there any other work for him but a good journal? We do not wish to know how his imaginary hero, but how he, the actual hero, lived from day to day."

journal. Later he might review what he had written, after adding "the most significant and poetic part. I do not know at first what charms me." Thoreau's double-distilled prose is at its strongest in short, taut passages: individual phrases, sentences, paragraphs. He was aware of this. In composing the final version of his journal, and the books quarried from it, he was concerned that the connecting links, if any, should be also of pure gold. Otherwise it was "better that the good be not united than that a bad man be admitted into their society." Thus in the early journals we get the sense that he was forever living in the moment, tuned to concert pitch, alert to capture the fleeting beauty of a world whose essence is impermanence. He could put all of New England spring into a single sentence: "Bluebirds' warbling curls in elms."

A poet, Thoreau believed, was one "who could impress the winds and streams into his service, to speak for him; who nailed words to their primitive senses." He used words as a cabinetmaker uses wood. He was in fact an expert carpenter, to the frequent benefit of literary friends like Emerson and Alcott. Late in life he fashioned a pine box to contain the many small notebooks that constituted his massive journal. Long after his death, when the manuscript journal was acquired by the Morgan Library, one row of notebooks appeared to fit a trifle loosely — a lapse, it would appear, from his standard of perfection. Not so. Research indicated that one notebook was missing. When it was recovered from a private dealer, it exactly filled the slot. His reputation was secure.

*   *   *

A year after Emerson had moved to Concord, he entertained overnight an odd visitor from Boston who was to become a close friend, disciple, and occasional object of charity: a philosopher whom even Thoreau would come to admire, despite their totally different views of man and the land. Bronson Alcott, born in 1799 (four years before Emerson) on a hill farm in Connecticut, a peddler and schoolteacher in his early years, had finally found an outlet for his radical views of education in the Temple School in Boston. But as Thoreau was ahead of his time in his attitude toward nature, so was Alcott in his understanding of the growing child. His methods were mocked, his idealism was seen a blasphemy, he was hooted in the streets, and his pupils melted away. When, after a brief flowering, his school failed, he decided to leave town for the country. "Concord seemed a desirable residence," he wrote in his journal for 1838, "as being near to Boston, healthful, and affording the society of my friend Mr. Emerson." He envied Emerson's rural surroundings: "I need the influence of Nature. The city does not whet my appetites and faculties." In 1840 he moved to the village that (except for one extended absence) was to be his home for the remainder of his long and troubled life.

Like Emerson and Thoreau, Alcott worshipped something called "Nature" — a word with as many individual interpretations as the word "God." Unlike his friends, however, he was neither a trained scholar nor a master craftsman in putting words on paper. Emerson refers to his "majestic utterances" (so inspiring that Emerson would forget the words) but Alcott's journals, which he kept so faithfully, resemble those of his friends only in their high-mindedness and their disregard of consistency. For a man brought up on a rock farm, he had a curiously idealistic concept of rural life, combined with a lack of practicality that often kept his family on the verge of starvation. Upon the one occasion when he did try to put his theories into practice — at Fruitlands in the nearby town of Harvard — the result was a tragic fiasco. Even Emerson, by nature sympathetic to this experiment in high thinking and communal living by Alcott and his friends, was skeptical from the start: "I will not prejudge them successful. They look well in July; we will see them in December." By December they had collapsed. Years later Alcott (who, incidentally, was away conducting "conversations" when the meager crops were ready for harvest) blamed the failure on the timing of the experiment. "It was undertaken too soon; the parties were all too unripe to sing and serve finely their song of a purely ideal life." As a farmer's son he might have added other causes: the late planting of the crops, the hours spent in arguing rather than hoeing, and the ban on the use of manure.

Soon after returning from Fruitlands, Alcott settled down with his wife and four daughters in a house on the old Lexington Road, a half-mile's stroll from Emerson's home at the corner of the new Cambridge Turnpike. Earlier, while writing *Nature* at the Old Manse, Emerson had paraphrased passages from Alcott's journals under the heading "What a certain Poet sang to me." And though he later remarked that "A. is a tedious archangel," he cherished the company of this self-centered mystic whose view of the natural world seems like an unintentional parody of his own. Emerson doubtless agreed with the comment: "I love nature much but man more." But Alcott would not stop there. Nature was "the Soul's cast off wardrobe." Man came first, nature is descended from him, mind is the source of all matter. This at a time when Lyell's *Principles of Geology* were well known, when Darwin was publishing *The Origin of Species*. At the Saturday Club in Boston, Bronson Alcott and the great naturalist Louis Agassiz met head on when Alcott claimed the "priority of Man and the animals to the earth." (Just where they resided before there was an earth is not clear.) The philosopher was unfazed by the arguments of a mere earthbound scientist. In any case (he noted in his journal), Agassiz's head-shape gave him away:

"Such breadth of brain and horizontal over-capping of the ears, globe-shaped, yet not ensphered nor astral, takes temperamentally to anatomic and mundane studies, to the forces and forms following, not leading, the sun."

Can this be the same person whom Henry Thoreau termed "the sanest man I ever knew," whom he welcomed for long evening talks at the hut on Walden Pond? The explanation lies, perhaps, in Alcott's all-embracing personality. Like Thoreau he sought to realize an entire life. He was a visionary who, in the words of his young friend, habitually took the farthest star and nebula into his scheme. "He has no creed. He is not pledged to any institution." Alcott in turn valued Thoreau as did few of his contemporaries: "A character of so much originality and probity of soul must prevail, and he is able and ready to wait his time." During one early spring evening at Walden, Thoreau, still quite unknown, read to Alcott passages from the manuscript of his first book, *A Week on the Concord and Merrimack Rivers.* Walking home at midnight on the snowy path through the woods, Alcott realized that here at last was a truly native talent. Its inspiration came

direct from the Concord countryside. "The book is purely American, fragrant with the lives of New England woods and streams, and could have been written nowhere else."

Yet in their attitudes toward the land itself, the two were poles apart. Theirs was a meeting of souls, not a meeting of minds. Alcott tried to share Thoreau's passion for wild nature, but it was uphill work. On the rare occasions when he joined his friends on an afternoon walk, he would perch on the first fence rail for a chat, and then be ready to go home. To him these were aimless wanderings. He would rather be pruning his apple trees and digging in his garden. (The only true gardener in the Concord group, he never learned to name even the common birds.) Thoreau praises wild apples, rhapsodizes over swamps, and even, Alcott complains, "defends the Indian from the doctrine of being lost or exterminated, and thinks that he holds a place between civilized man and nature, and must hold it. I say he goes along with the woods and the beasts, who retreat before and are superseded by man and the planting of orchards and gardens."

To give Alcott some congenial busywork while he himself was abroad, Emerson commissioned a summerhouse for his garden. This was Alcott's dish of tea. "Whatever the eye can do, I am good for." He went to work with creative rapture. No nonsense about wild nature here. This would be a bower where the bard would entertain the muses; there would be nine joists, one for each muse. The design, entirely Alcott's own, featured curved rafters meeting at the ridgepole and "bending brackets depending thereon as if to find the ground and take root therein." His plan would demonstrate the fitness of the curve over the straight line. "The serpentine is ever mystic." Thoreau, who accepted mysticism but liked straight lines, reluctantly lent a hand with the building, admitting in a letter to Emerson, "I feel a little oppressed when I come near it. It has no great dis-

position to be beautiful." The townspeople were less re-
strained. Alcott, unabashed, records their comments: " 'It
is odd,' 'The strangest thing I ever saw,' 'A whirligig,' etc.,
etc. . ." "The finest work of M. Angelo," he notes defiantly,
"set in the market place, would doubtless provoke as many
and as alien remarks."

This absurd structure seems symbolic. As his biographer
Odell Shepard remarks, Bronson Alcott was at heart a
classicist. Despite his homage to naturalism (those curves
and rooting brackets), nature unshaped by man meant
little to him. The Musketaquid or Concord River, which
fired the imagination of Thoreau and Emerson and Channing, and Hawthorne in his early days, was a place for a
picnic and nothing more. Forget the wilderness, the savage
past. Concord he saw as "a classic land." Though its poets
were associated with the fields and forest and lakes and
rivers of the township, it was — and always had been — a
civilized American village, settled by Englishmen: a symbol to Alcott of man's victory over nature and over the
brute beast in himself.

*   *   *

"Between two tall gate-posts of rough-hewn stone . . . we
beheld the grey front of the old parsonage, terminating the
vista of an avenue of black-ash trees. It was now a twelve-
month since the funeral procession of the venerable clergyman, its last inhabitant, had turned from that gateway
towards the village burying-ground." In July of 1842
Nathaniel Hawthorne — a year Emerson's junior — had
married Sophia Peabody and brought his bride to the Old
Manse, for what would be the three happiest years of his
life. Here was the "most delightful little nook of a study,"
from the north window of which one looked out on the
scene of the Concord fight. Here William Emerson's successor, the late "venerable clergyman," Ezra Ripley, "had

penned nearly three thousand discourses," and here William's grandson, Ralph Waldo, had written *Nature* only a
few years before. For Hawthorne the best feature of the
study was the view through the small cracked panes of the
two west windows, which gave on an old orchard with
glimpses of the river through the trees. At last, after years
of brooding solitude in Salem, he had a wife and a home.

Like Alcott, Hawthorne had been attracted to Concord by
the presence of Emerson, who was now living in the big
square house at the other end of town. Son of a Salem sea
captain, a graduate of Bowdoin College, he had happily run
wild during childhood summers on his uncle's large tract
of land in northern Maine. The novels of Walter Scott had
whetted his appetite for the not dissimilar scenery of New
England. At first he had been a bit supercilious about the
sluggish stream at the foot of his orchard; compared to the
mighty Penobscot River and the Maine lakes, it seemed
pretty tame. But he soon capitulated. "Perhaps, like other
gentle and quiet characters, it will be better appreciated,

the longer I am acquainted with it." One evening at sunset, looking out from the hill opposite the Manse, he felt
that the Concord landscape had a quiet beauty in keeping
with the river. The white village appeared to be em-
bosomed among the wooded hills, the broad meadows lent
"a secure homeliness" to the scene.

Fresh from a brief experience in the uncongenial atmosphere of Brook Farm, fed up with reformers and communal living, Hawthorne saw his Concord hideaway as a
Garden of Eden, in which he and his bride might live in
deep and quiet rapture. Like Emerson, he came to Concord
with a determination to do nothing against his own genius.
The immediate temptation was to do nothing at all. By his
own admission, he hated all labor, but less that of the hands
than of the head. He had inherited Ezra Ripley's fruit trees
and vegetable plot; gardening was easier work than writing. The journal which he kept in obedience to his beloved
Sophia abounds in half-humorous allusions to the glory of
a field of Indian corn, the delicacy of young beans hidden
among the foliage, or the classic beauty of a summer squash.
"The natural taste of man for the original Adam's occupa-
tion is fast developing itself in me." From his retreat the
competitive world outside seemed like a dream. "My business," he wrote, "is merely to live and to enjoy" — an unconscious echo of young Henry Thoreau's defiant statement
that the world is more to be enjoyed than used. Nevertheless, despite his claims to indolence, Hawthorne wrote some
of his best short stories during this first sojourn in Concord.

Throughout his voluminous and enchanting notebooks
for these years are shrewd, affectionate, irreverent por-
traits of his contemporaries who were seeking inspiration in
the Concord countryside. Worldlier than they, he could
view them with the same amused detachment that he applied to himself. Emerson would occasionally call at the
Manse, accompanied perhaps by that "gnome, yclept El-

lery Channing... One of those queer and clever young men whom Mr. Emerson (that everlasting rejecter of all that is, and seeker for he knows not what) is continually picking up by way of a genius." As for Emerson himself, he and Hawthorne, despite their friendship, never really understood each other. The cool, controlled seeker after light was blind to the shadows among which Hawthorne lived. Shortly after the latter had come to Concord, Emerson noted in his journal, "Nathaniel Hawthorne's reputation as a writer is a very pleasing fact, because his writing is not good for anything, and this is a tribute to the man." Handsome, with deep-set eyes and long curling lashes, loosejointed, never robust, Hawthorne appeared to Emerson to have a feminine cast of mind. "Alcott and he together would make a man."

Oddly enough it was Henry Thoreau, that worshiper of the wild, with whom this domesticated, home-loving genius had the closest rapport. "Mr. Thorow* dined with us yesterday. He is a singular character — a young man [Thoreau was then twenty-five] with much of wild original nature still remaining in him ... Ugly as sin, long-nosed, queer-mouthed, with uncouth and somewhat rustic, although courteous, manners ... His ugliness is of an honest and agreeable fashion, and becomes him much better than beauty." Hawthorne envied Thoreau his intimacy with the natural world, his powers of observation comparable to the insights of an original poet. To hear him talk was "like hearing the wind among the boughs of a forest-tree." As together they walked the banks of the Concord River, Hawthorne could not but feel a deeper intimacy with the living landscape than he had ever known before. Needing money, Thoreau sold his new friend his boat, the *Musketaquid* (built for the now-famous journey on the Concord and

* This should settle the question of how Thoreau pronounced his name. Elsewhere there is a punning comparison to the word "thorough."

Merrimack) for seven dollars, and patiently tried to teach him how to manage it in the current. "I wish," wrote Hawthorne ruefully after the first lesson, "that I could acquire the aquatic skill of its original owner at as reasonable a rate." He rechristened his craft the *Water Lily* and was soon able to paddle it alone against wind and current to the lower reaches of the North Branch or Assabet. Never had he conceived that there could be so remote and beautiful a river scene in Concord. He was entranced by the trees stretching their arms to the very surface of the water, by the twining vines and the sunlight filtering through the canopy, and most of all by the reflections as he gazed downward and saw the foliage and sky "arrayed in ideal beauty, which satisfied the spirit incomparably more than the actual scene." How much more beautiful was reflection than what we call reality. To Hawthorne, such scenes were symbolic of the human condition. Tragically aware of man's grossness and impurity, he took comfort in the thought "that even a human breast which may appear least spiritual in some aspects, may still have the capability of reflecting an infinite Heaven in its depths."

In his lighter moments, Hawthorne responded to his rural surroundings with a playfulness unthinkable in his transcendental friends. Floundering through the underbrush on his way to return a book to Emerson, he disturbs a company of crows in the tree tops; he feels for a moment as if he had broken the peace of the Sabbath. "A crow, however, has no real pretensions to religion, in spite of their gravity of mien and black attire; — they are certainly thieves, and probably infidels." Seeking a bouquet of flowers for his wife, he spies a fragrant water lily growing near the riverbank but "with sweet prudishness, beyond the grasp of mortal arm. But it does not escape me so." He wades in after it, heedless of wet pantaloons. "I know what is its fitting destiny, better than the silly flower knows for

itself." He twits himself about his invariable custom of
getting lost in the woods — emerging on the Walden road
and confidently walking off in the opposite direction from
town. Yet underneath this banter there is a yearning for
something that he will never achieve. "Oh that I could run
wild! — that is, that I could put myself into a true relation
with nature, and be on friendly terms with all congenial
elements."

The concept of wild nature did in fact profoundly influence Hawthorne's writing in some of its greatest passages.
But his was not the friendly and congenial reality that
Thoreau sought on his afternoon walks through Concord
and Lincoln. Still less was it the idealized, abstract concept
that Emerson shaped and polished in his study, calmly
turning each facet to the light. In Hawthorne's stories we
find the dark brooding nightmare forest of the early Puritans, the heathen wilderness that surrounds every village,
and every human soul. Here young Goodman Brown kept
his tryst with the Devil, amid "the creaking of the trees,

and howling of wild beasts, the yell of Indians . . . as if all Nature were laughing him to scorn." Here, where the witches held their Sabbath, Hester Prynne met her lover and cast away her scarlet letter. For a brief moment, Nature — "that wild, heathen Nature of the forest, never subjected by human law, nor illuminated by higher truth" — smiled upon their love; but as Hester resumed the symbol of her shame the sunlight faded and the gray shadows returned. So Hawthorne, who complained about the difficulty of writing romances in a country "where there is no shadow, no antiquity, no mystery, no picturesque and gloomy wrong," looked back to a time in America when untamed nature was a symbol of evil. The gentle, sunlit countryside of Concord nourished his spirit; it permeates his notebooks and finds loving expression in such essays as the introduction to *Mosses from an Old Manse*. But the haunted landscape of his romances derives less from the world about him than from his own dark dreams and tragic sense of life.

*   *   *

During his stay at Brook Farm, Hawthorne had come into contact with one of the most formidable characters ever to set foot in Concord. Margaret Fuller, Emerson's passionate and unsettling disciple, had like Emerson himself refused to join the Brook Farm community, but she was a constant visitor. Hawthorne lampooned her in his description of a refractory animal dubbed the Transcendental Heifer, who was "very fractious" and "apt to kick over the milk pail. . . She is not an amiable cow; but she has a very intelligent face, and seems to be of a reflective cast of character." Plain of feature, "monstrously learned" (she was the first woman allowed to use the Harvard Library), Miss Fuller was sometimes lacking in sensitivity. Hawthorne and Sophia had no sooner found their quiet haven in the

Old Manse than she suggested that her newlywed sister Ellen and husband Ellery Channing move in with them. Hawthorne was polite but appalled: "Had it been proposed to Adam and Eve to receive two angels in their Paradise, as *boarders*, I doubt whether they would have been altogether pleased to consent."

A former assistant (with Sophia Hawthorne's sister, Elizabeth Peabody) to Bronson Alcott at the Temple School, an organizer of "conversations" among Boston's intellectual women, editor of the *Dial*, Margaret Fuller, unlike Emerson, felt no need to reject the city for the peace of a country village. Yet she was a house guest of the Emersons for weeks at a time. A forthright liberal and battler for women's rights, she spoke for a rebellious generation intent on doing their "thing."

Margaret Fuller shared the transcendentalists' romantic view of Nature; Emerson's little book by that name was her Bible. But she protested against those who "go to an extreme in [their] denunciations of cities and the social institutions." Today her words have a modern ring: "When we get the proper perspective on these things we shall find man, however artificial, still a part of Nature." Though a city person at heart, miserable when deprived of intellectual companionship, she sometimes yearned for wildness. The countryside around Groton, to which her father had moved the family, struck her as "very beautiful in its way" but "too tamely smiling and sleepy." Eager to see frontier America, she joined her friend James Freeman Clarke and his sister in a trip west. They got as far as Wisconsin, and Margaret went on to the island of Mackinaw, where she made trips into the wilderness alone with Indian guides, calmly taking the risks of shooting the rapids in a canoe. Fascinated with the Indian way of life, she was revolted by their corruption at the hands of the traders and the missionaries, and the desecration of the lovely land that once was theirs: "We feel as if they were the rightful lords of a beauty they forebore to deform." The journal of this western trip became her first book, *Summer on the Lakes in 1843*: a potpourri that encouraged Thoreau to put together his similarly discursive *A Week on the Concord and Merrimack Rivers*.

Emerson listed Thoreau as one of Margaret Fuller's "enemies"; she had consistently rejected his submissions when she was editor of the *Dial*. Yet their responses to nature were often much alike. "Every sight is worth twice as much by the early morning light," she writes on her western trip. "We borrow something of the spirit of the hour to look upon them." In a little waterfall near Niagara, she sees "a study for some larger design," as Thoreau would later in Sawmill Brook. After she had moved to New York, she used a book review to castigate those who write in an "apologetic tone for hours passed in the contemplation of natural beauty. . . Let those 'erring brethren' apologize who spend their lives in gossip, or money-making; not those who think it worth while to devote some hours to sympathy with the glories that surround them."

Her appreciation of these "glories" went beyond the superficial romanticism of her time and, in its sophistication, probably beyond that of her more famous Concord companions. Writing from London, three years before her untimely death, she contrasts the late paintings of Turner with "the English gentleman's conventional view of Nature, which implies a *little* sentiment and a *very* cultivated taste. He has become awake to what is elemental, normal, in Nature."

*   *   *

Never has the writer's debt to nature been more eloquently acknowledged than it was by the Concord group. "Group," however, is a misnomer. Emerson, Thoreau, Alcott, Hawthorne, Margaret Fuller — Ellery Channing and Jones Very and the other "clever young men" attracted to the light that shone from Emerson's study window — can one conceive of a more disparate collection of passionate individualists? They stimulated one another, occasionally exasperated one another, appreciated and criticized one another's ideas in their journals, and were quick to offer a helping hand — be it Thoreau spading their gardens for Emerson and Hawthorne, or the latter, as established authors, assisting their young friend to get his early work into print. But no two of them responded in the same way to the Concord countryside; each distilled his own brand of truth from the natural world about him.

Henry Thoreau's distillate was of course the most potent and the most lasting. As Alcott said, he was willing to wait his time, and his time has come. His attitude toward the land, so different from that of the first settlers, was even more at odds with the ruthless exploitation that had already begun in his lifetime. Almost too late, we are beginning to listen to him. Yet he is still far ahead of us. He knew the fallacy of regarding the land as merely marketable property. He deplored "this war with the wilderness," in which the pine tree is regarded as an enemy. With extraordinary foresight, he declared that "each town should have a park, or rather a primitive forest, of five hundred or a thousand acres, where a stick should never be cut for fuel, a common possession forever, for instruction and recreation. . . Let us keep the New World *new*, preserve all the advantages of living in the country. Walden Wood and the Easterbrooks [Estabrook] country should be protected forever."*

Thoreau's concern reached beyond the borders of Concord and Lincoln to the nation and the globe itself. "Why

* Walden is now a state park and is being restored more nearly to its condition in Thoreau's day. Much of the Estabrook Woods (the abandoned farms are now almost all grown up to forest) has been acquired as a natural research area by Harvard University's Museum of Comparative Zoology.

should not we, who have renounced the king's authority, have our national preserves . . . our forests, not to hold the king's game merely, but to hold and preserve the king himself also, the lord of creation — not for idle sport or food, but for inspiration, and our own true recreation?" "What is the use of a house," he wrote to a friend toward the end of his life, "if you haven't got a tolerable planet to put it on?"

If we still have a tolerable planet, much credit can go to the revolutionary ideas about man's place in nature expressed by a few writers of genius living in the quiet valley of the Musketaquid — most of all by Henry Thoreau himself, whose purpose was nothing less than to express in word and act the "perfect correspondence of Nature to man." The measure of his success is the avidity with which his words are now being read and his principles (notably among the young) being put into practice. For Thoreau's massive Journal still comprises the best case history we possess of one man's attempt to live in harmony with the land.

CHAPTER 14 ⌐

"[We must] quit thinking about decent land-use as solely an economic problem. . . A thing is right when it tends to preserve the integrity, stability, and beauty of the biotic community. It is wrong when it tends otherwise."
— Aldo Leopold

Two Worlds Meet

When Emerson published his embattled little book, *Nature*, in 1836, the white man had been reshaping the face of the Concord region for two hundred years. By and large, the process was unremarked, taken for granted, a by-product of the dawn-to-dusk business of making a living off the land. In setting out his orchard, the Lincoln farmer was thinking of winter apples and hard cider, not of esthetic appeal; his pleasant pastures and rippling fields of corn were to feed his cows, not to look at. What Emerson, the poet, called the best of his farm grew out of a happy marriage of natural topography and intelligent, thrifty use of the land — for the farmer was also thinking of his children and grandchildren. But already during Emerson's lifetime this agrarian way of life, which had produced such an esthetically pleasing landscape, was beginning to decline. In her *Changing Face of New England*, Betty Flanders Thomson mentions the widespread alarm that this caused among those who saw the farmer as the very core of our national tradition. Throughout the 1880s and 1890s the popular magazines had "articles written from all points of view, impassioned, reasoned, or merely sentimental, setting forth proposals for keeping people on the farms in order to preserve our Great Heritage of plain living and high thinking, and of course in an idyllic rural setting."

As urban New England grew and flourished, young men

everywhere left their native villages for careers in business, in manufacturing, in law, in medicine, in the ministry — but traditionally (in Lincoln at least) one son stayed at home to manage the family farm. What would happen when this tradition died, when the land, however lovingly tilled for generations, became more valuable for house lots than for crops; when the inevitable pressure for "improvements" — be they waterworks or street railways or electric lights or whatever — threatened to force city standards on a simple country town? Being so near to Boston, Lincoln had even before the turn of the century begun to experience the shock waves of two worlds in collision.

The comic aspects of Lincoln's initial encounter with the blessings of modern technology, though recognized at the time, were more apparent to later generations, who did not have to pay the bill. As far back as 1856, when the town was barely more than a century old, it had been faced with a threat from outside to its most vital possession: its water supply. The town meeting for that year, alarmed by claims to Lincoln water by the Cambridge Water Works, appointed a commission to appear before the state legislature "and if it be the purpose of the City of Cambridge or any other persons to obtain any interest or control of the waters of the forest Lake known as Flints or Sandy Pond in the Town of Lincoln [they shall] do all in their power to defend the interests of the Town . . ." The Cambridge officials apparently backed down. However, a greater threat lay close to home. A law passed in 1872 authorized Concord as well as Lincoln to take water from Sandy Pond. If ever there was not enough for both, Lincoln would have first rights. But apparently the far-sighted town fathers realized that a growing community could not depend forever on private wells, and feared that if they had no waterworks of their own, their more populous neighbor would some day pre-empt the pond for itself. And so the town, with a financial boldness quite out of character, plunged headlong into an expensive project which, in the words of Charles Francis Adams, for thirty years "not only supplied a portion of the community with water, but the whole of it with an ever-present bone of unfailing contention."

The story of the Lincoln Water Works has a mock-heroic quality; it is a village saga that would have delighted Mrs. Gaskell or Anthony Trollope. The Lincoln taxpayers, however, did not find it so quaint. At an ultimate cost of some forty thousand dollars, a small reservoir was built on top of the hill, a pumping engine and pipes installed on Sandy Pond, and the water was ready to flow. But to whom? Most of Lincoln's 800 residents were widely scattered; only a handful lived close enough to the center to enjoy this modern improvement. Their fees would never pay for pumping the water, and the town refused to do so. Thus within a few months of completion the fine new works were shut down, and the Water Commissioners' annual report concluded with a sour epitaph: "If a farmer had a cow or a horse which cost him five or six times as much to keep as the income he could get from it, he would not need to study the situation long. He would dispose of the animal if he could find someone having more faith in poverty than he, or failing in that, bury it..."

Bury it, however, they could not, with interest to pay on the investment and two lawsuits aimed at compelling them to keep pumping. Whether out of faith or desperation, a committee of water takers assumed responsibility for what the Selectmen referred to as "an elephant, and a dead one at that." Ten years later, having received no revenue, the town took the elephant back, meanwhile having grudgingly settled one of the lawsuits. The lawyer for the plaintiff — the Selectman reported resignedly — was young, handsome, and eloquent. "When he depicted the hardheartedness of town officers, and touched upon the wrongs of the widow and fatherless, one might almost see the tears fall and hear the children crying for bread, and the bewildered jurymen, what could they do? They did just as other juries do, decided the town must pay."

Such was Lincoln's first, expensive experience with civic progress. The works were finally paid for and water now flows throughout most of the town. While the battle lasted, it generated both bitterness and homespun humor.

*   *   *

The epic water controversy was but a portent of greater changes to come. When the new town hall was dedicated in 1892, an elderly guest — born and raised in Lincoln and having returned for the ceremonies — remarked that "this town has, in a manner, reached a turning of the ways. Changes have taken place within it during the past few years greater than for a long period in its previous history . . . As I view these buildings [the "stone church," the new town hall, and the library had all been built during the previous decade], as I look over this audience, I see not the Lincoln of my boyhood." Yet ten years later a reporter from the Boston *Herald* described Lincoln as a peculiar town in that "it doesn't want to be considered up-to-date." He quoted a Lincoln gentleman as saying: "We have a little, quiet, country town, and we want to keep it just that and nothing more."*

The gentleman's quiet country town was, however, no longer the farm village that the elderly Lincolnian had looked back on with nostalgia, and the difference lay deeper than the new and elegant buildings that had so altered the appearance of Lincoln Hill. The gentleman being interviewed was well-to-do and made his money in Boston. For him, Lincoln was a refuge from the noise and bustle of the

---

* In 1888, the Board of Selectmen reported with a certain complacency: "Nothing of importance — save a suicide by drowning and an occasional house-break — has occurred during the year to mar the tranquillity of this, in other respects, the most quiet and peaceful of towns. Entertaining all due respect for what may have been published in the Record in favor of other towns as being the most desirable place to live in, in our opinion Lincoln, by merit, is entitled to the prize."

city, the glare of electric lights and the rattle of streetcars. He had a sophisticated appreciation of pastoral beauty: the land was an important part of his life, but it was not his living. His was one of a number of country estates, in contrast to working farms, that grew up in Lincoln around the turn of the century. Most of them were owned by business or professional men who in many cases enjoyed Lincoln simply as a summer (or spring and fall) home, attracted there not only by the beauty of the countryside but by a tax rate which, at around eight dollars per thousand, was one of the lowest in Massachusetts. But if taxes were low, land values were steadily rising, foreshadowing the day when only the more prosperous farmers could afford to hold and work their acres, when they could realize so much more money by selling out and starting elsewhere. Thus Lincoln began to acquire the reputation of a rich man's town. No matter that the wealth was confined to a few families and was unobtrusive. (A proper Bostonian would never allow himself to be seen in public with his deposit slip showing.) The comparatively brief period of the big estates provided newspaper writers with a stereotype which is still dusted off from time to time for fresh articles about the wealthy Boston suburbs.

In 1900 a local controversy arose that was a feature writer's dream. All over the country, electric streetcar companies were booming, and the Boston area was no exception. "GLOBE EXTRA! LINCOLN EXCITED. Turmoil Over Proposed Coming of a Street Railway. 'Aristocrats' and 'Farmers' Issue Lively Circulars — Class Feeling Runs High." For the first time in its history, Lincoln was in danger of being split along both class and geographical lines. The explosion was touched off by an anti-railway circular addressed to the voters by a group of conservative, and in several cases wealthy, citizens, some of them newcomers to Lincoln. They feared that streetcars would destroy the rural character of the town, bringing in "rowdies" from the city, eventually driving out the big landowners and devaluing real estate. Most of the signers lived in the center or in South Lincoln. A group from North Lincoln replied with fury, using the issue as an occasion to air their pent-up resentments on several scores. "We have no lights, no water, and no means of getting our children to high school in Concord. None of us have coachmen. . ." Cheap access to the Boston markets, they went on, may mean little to the rich, "but to us who earn our money by honest work the saving of 50 cents is considerable." The circular ended with a parting shot: "If our new citizens want war, let them remember that the north part of town is an old battleground and we believe that our fighting blood is as good as ever." In reply, the so-called "aristocrats" pointed out that there were newcomers on both sides of the quarrel, and that many who opposed the railway, including all three Selectmen, were farmers.

The issue was, in fact, more complex than these angry outbursts would suggest, and of general concern beyond the borders of Lincoln. It was a burning question in many towns. The hastily organized street railway companies, oblivious to the need for orderly land development, were flooding the state legislature with bills allowing them to use existing highways and to purchase private rights of way for their tracks, with competing lines perhaps running side by side. One of the worst bills called for running a track through the center of Lincoln and, for the purpose of attracting customers, building "places of amusement" on Sandy and Walden Ponds. Instead, however, of blindly opposing all street railways, Lincoln's Selectmen drew up a masterful document which came to be known as the "Lincoln bill" and was generally accepted as a model. It gave to each town exclusive right to control the route of the railway and to take land for the purpose. Two years later the Lincoln Selectmen did in fact lay out a way for "electric roads" through North Lincoln. Perhaps the lack of provision for amusement parks made it unattractive to the promoters. At any rate, the cars never came, and rural Lincoln was given a reprieve — without a civil war.

*　　*　　*

Though the rich newcomers to Lincoln may have been resented in some quarters, the town's official stance was one of warm welcome, not to say subtle allurement. When the new town hall was finished, the Common was spruced up by regrading, trimming trees, and so on, with an eye to attracting outsiders. "Improvements are noticed by strangers, as well as by townspeople," reported the Selectmen. "First impressions go a great way toward securing new and desirable residents, who increase our wealth and lessen our taxes."

Dr. Edward W. Emerson, Ralph Waldo's grandson, offered a word of advice to newcomers during Lincoln's hundred and fiftieth anniversary celebrations: "Now to the new settlers may I say, Do not come to Lincoln to enjoy its quiet, its air, and its scenery, and lead your lives apart from it. Live in a simple country town in simple country ways, and don't spoil the place by enhancing class distinctions and living in a style which may make your neighbors uncomfortable. . . Come into sound and helpful touch with town affairs."

However, one new resident who swelled the tax rolls enjoyed his wealth less quietly than Dr. Emerson might have wished. In his reminiscences, the sporting son of the founder of the Boston Symphony Orchestra recalls how the fields and woods of Lincoln once echoed to the sound of his horn. His father bought him a fine old farm, and with a pack of choice foxhounds imported from England he established the Middlesex Hunt. At first he believed that the New England countryside was too cramped for anything but a drag hunt: too much covert, too many swamps, too few foxes. But his huntsman — recommended by none less than an English duke — persuaded him that rural Lincoln "could show good sport with fox-hounds, hunting the real animal." Moreover, the town was "very fortunate in having an excellent class of landowners who enjoy the sport and are justly proud of its pack and its prowess all over the country." With the arrival of the motorcar, however, Lincoln's brief encounter with blood sports came to an end, for the American motorist, he remarked regretfully, "is not trained, like his British cousin, to stop when he sees hounds on the highway."

Over the years, Lincoln's wealthier families — whether newcomers or older residents — have thought of the town as more than a convenient place to hunt foxes or enjoy the country air. Many of them cared enough for it to become substantial benefactors. They had an early precedent in the trust fund of 388 pounds, 10 shillings, and 5 pence, established in 1761 by Joseph Brooks (the same who gave the bell for the first meetinghouse) for maintenance of a school. The town library, as we have seen, was born when the widow of a distinguished professor provided books, and a successful businessman a building to house them. Shortly thereafter, a copper magnate from an old Lincoln family left a sizable sum for a new town hall and for a series of public lectures "of an instructive and elevating character" to be delivered in it — and delivered they have been to this day, providing free instruction, elevation, and entertainment three or four times a year, of a quality that a large city foundation might envy. A farm built on Lincoln's largest drumlin has become the headquarters of the Massachusetts Audubon Society, devoted not only to ornithology and conservation but, thanks to the foresight of the donor, to giving busloads of children from the inner city a chance to see where milk and eggs come from and to enjoy hayrides behind great draft horses like those that once pulled the plow in Lincoln fields. Other bequests, less prescient of future needs, have had strings attached to them that only the

courts could untangle. Many years were consumed in dealing with a bequest for a town hearse, and with donations to
the "silent poor," described as "that class of honest temperate men and women who work hard or who are prudent
and economical and yet find it hard to make both ends
meet." A fine building and grounds left for an unneeded
hospital were eventually diverted by legal action to other
town purposes, as was also a bequest for a high school,
which became unnecessary as regional schools were developed.

But the splendid gift horse that had to be looked most
firmly in the mouth was a red brick castle overlooking
Sandy Pond. This was the summer house and private museum of Julian de Cordova, self-styled Conde de Cabra,
Marquis of Almadovar. A wealthy businessman and speculator with an insatiable passion for travel, an omniverous
collector of "everything that took my fancy in every country in the world," de Cordova was also a dreamer determined to make his dreams come true. And so he did, in the
fantastic, turreted pile built on the hilltop overlooking the
pond where Thoreau had once wished to build his cabin.
"Look at the view from this balcony," de Cordova said
proudly. "That's Sandy Pond down there, the water supply of Lincoln, but to me, a times, it seems like the Gen-
eraliffe Gardens just across from the valley of the Alham-
bra." The old icehouse he converted into a Swiss chalet,
and on the lakeshore he built a bright orange oriental tea-
house. The feature of the garden was a rocky flume and an
illuminated star-shaped fountain built of glass doorknobs
from the glass factory whence much of his fortune was derived. Inside the castle were crowded picture galleries, a
Moorish room, an oriental room, ornate carving, and inlaid
furniture, countless "antiques," a miniature Taj Mahal,
and a "miracle mirror" that flashed a hidden image of
Buddha on the ceiling.

Lincoln had never seen the like. With a generous instinct

to share his treasure, and real love for the town where his dreams had been realized, de Cordova opened his estate to the public and later bequeathed it to his fellow townsmen for a museum and park. Alas, when he died at the age of ninety-five, a professional appraiser of his lifelong acquisitions declared them "utterly worthless from any museum point of view," and recommended tearing down the castle and erecting in its stead a community center for the arts. The resultant legal battle between trustees and the town was finally resolved in favor of the latter, in what was to become a landmark decision. The castle still stands, gutted, rebuilt; within the old shell is a highly respected modern museum. It was a clever metamorphosis of one man's fantasy into a public institution that preserved his memory in a way that even this greatest of dreamers could never have conceived. Julian de Cordova had not exactly followed Dr. Emerson's admonition to live in simple country ways, but in his unique manner he became a local legend, while to thousands of visitors from the city and surrounding towns, "Lincoln" means the De Cordova Museum.

The era of the great estates was a brief episode in Lincoln's long history, but it had a lasting effect on the landscape by saving open space until such time as the town government was ready to meet pressures from the city with long-range planning. The same newspaper reporter who interviewed the country getleman in 1902 was himself struck by "the immense amount of territory set apart as woodland or laid down to grass," by how comparatively little was under cultivation. This did not mean that the farmers had all succumbed to rising land prices and sold out. It did mean that the new type of commercial farming mentioned earlier — the intensive cultivation of a small area — had already changed the pattern of land use and apparently changed the farmer's way of life as well. "The town being but fifteen miles from Boston and a quick market," wrote a journalist in the early nineties, "the old style of farming has passed away and market gardening, with hothouses and acres of early vegetables and small fruits, has transformed the old true farmer into a shrewd business man, with his city cousin's habit of economizing time and driving business from early dawn until far beyond sunset."

Twenty years later, a Boston newspaper described Lincoln as "a little town, known for its many fine residences. . . On many of the large estates, farming is carried on extensively." The wealthy newcomers had introduced a new element into the Lincoln scene: the gentleman farmer. Their prize herds of Guernsey and Jersey cows, their saddle horses, their flocks of fancy sheep all played a part in maintaining the pastures and meadows and long open vistas that are the hallmark of a true New England landscape, in contrast to the suburban pattern of well-mowed lawns surrounded by third-growth forest. The same article states that, among the number of clubs, lodges, and other organizations that have meeting places in the town, "the most prominent of them is the Lincoln Grange, Patrons of Husbandry, which has a hall in South Lincoln" — and which remains an active organization to this day.

As it entered the twentieth century, Lincoln may still have been a little town, but it could no longer be called a rural village. It was already facing pressures from the urban world that required, to be dealt with effectively, a high degree of sophistication on the part of the town fathers. The crusty character who earlier remarked at town meeting that "one farmer is worth more than six lawyers" might have changed his mind had he known the complex issues that lay ahead.

Probably the most active force that shapes the growth of any town is its means of access to other communities. In the case of New England towns this meant first wilderness trails, then rough roads (supplemented for a while by canals), then railroads, finally motor highways. The first decisive event to alter the way of life in Lincoln was the completion of the Fitchburg Railroad in 1844. The second was the epening of the new Concord Turnpike ninety years later.

Before the days of Henry Ford, when motorcars were as much pleasure craft as motorboats, they had little impact on daily life in Lincoln (with the exception of the huntsmen who resented their indifference to foxhounds on the highway). Town officials, however, adopted a hard line in protecting residents from the menace of speeding vehicles. Their attitude toward motorists reminds one of Mrs. Patrick Campbell's comment on the morals of the lower classes: Let them do what they like, so long as they don't do it in the streets and frighten the horses. In the summer of 1902, the chairman of the Selectmen of Lincoln printed a "Notice to Automobilists" warning them that the maximum speed on a town highway was eight miles per hour, reduced to three when passing a rider or horsedrawn vehicle. Defiant motorists refused to obey, since the state speed limit was fifteen. So one Sunday, it is reported, "the town officers measured off a course on one of the much-frequented roads, and stationing a man with a tin horn at one end, placed another man with a stop watch at the other, and just beyond the second man stretched a rope across the road. Ogden Codman, Jr., of Lincoln soon came along on a motorcycle which he was running, so the officers said, at the rate of eighteen miles per hour. The officers say that they signalled him to stop but that he paid no attention. At any rate, he ran into the rope, got a bad fall and a big bruise." A rough way, one would think, to treat a descendant of Lincoln's founding father. Virtually alone in its conservatism, Lincoln eventually had to go along with the rest of the state, comforted perhaps by the movement to license drivers of these dangerous machines and to require that there "be some distinguishing mark on every horseless carriage which goes on the road."

When Ogden Codman, Jr., had his great fall, the Boston-Concord Turnpike had been in existence for almost a century. Built by a chartered company, it was originally a toll road, on which the stagecoach traveled thrice a week, making the journey in three hours if the weather was fair and the roadbed smooth. (Broad cartwheels helped to keep the road in shape. By law, "carts or waggons with wheel fellies six inches wide" paid only half the toll.) These old turnpikes reflected a mania for straight lines, and generally went directly through the center of the towns they served.

The Cambridge (or Boston) Turnpike, which ran by Emerson's front door, remained essentially in its same location until 1934, exactly a hundred years after the sage had moved to Concord. Now a fine new highway, rebuilt at the cost of three million dollars, would bypass Concord on its way west. As originally planned, however, it would have cut right through the center of Lincoln. Fortunately an influential townsman and state representative redirected the flow of concrete, and Lincoln Hill was saved. But the new road brought the cities of both Cambridge and Boston within quick and easy reach, at any hour of the day or night. Lincoln had become, at long last, a part of "suburbia."

CHAPTER 15 ⌐

"There is no need to accept a future of blanketing urbanization in which individuals and communities lose their identity."
— *The Use of Land*, edited by William K. Reilly, 1973

"Ecology is the new thing nowadays. I don't know if you have it yet, out West. It's the same thing as Conservation, and you have to have it, or else Nature will just be crawling all over you."
— Unidentified lady, Connecticut, 1972

Room for Living

What does it mean to be a "suburb"? The word itself, from the Latin *suburbium*, is as old as Rome. In the early nineteenth century, it was employed by Lord Byron in a pejorative sense: "vulgar, dowdyish, and suburban" (in reference to the environs of London). Today it has a variety of connotations: at the one extreme the gridiron development of flimsy houses and postage stamp lawns; at the other, country clubs and landscaped estates. Communities like Lincoln, with a long history as independent towns, obviously fit into neither category. But where do they fit? What is the function of the suburb in an increasingly urban society?

It is not, in any case, simply to extend the city limits by providing more bedrooms, more shopping centers, more paved roads to transport more commuters to a city center. Ideally, as mentioned at the beginning of this book, the self-respecting and far-sighted suburban town, with a sense of pride in community, is one of the best means of preventing urban sprawl. In biological terms, a chief function of a suburb like Lincoln is to serve as the city's lungs, to give it a chance to breathe. It is to preserve, within reach of city dwellers, clear air and clean waters, birdsong and the smell of wet earth, sunlit fields and quiet woods where one may enjoy "green thoughts in a green shade." It is to forestall the complete divorce of man from nature which must otherwise result from the steady drain of our population away from the land, into the metropolitan areas.

In 1934, when I came with my family to Lincoln, we knew little of its history. It was the landscape, the physical appearance of the town, that attracted us. How this rural quality had been preserved, we had no idea; probably we were not even aware that it was threatened. Only after living here awhile did we come to realize that such matters do not take care of themselves, that Lincoln is what it is not through chance but through wise planning and hard work.

The point was brought politely to our attention on a spring morning in 1938. After renting for four years, we had acquired sixteen acres of rolling pasture and woodlot, with a farm cottage that we could convert into an adequate house. My wife and I were happily watching the carpenters complete their work when we were joined by a mild-mannered man who introduced himself as a member of the town's newly created Planning Board. He looked on silently while the last of the shingles were nailed to the roof-tree. "I suppose you want to go ahead with it?" he inquired gently. I allowed that we did. He then explained that the town had recently passed a bylaw requiring official approval of "subdivisions." The man from whom we bought the land had been quite unaware of any such regulation — which was, in fact, being exercised for the first time. The town officers were understanding. Hearings were promptly held, imaginary "paper roads" were laid out as required by law (giving access to the backland should it ever be developed), and we became legitimate.

In those days Lincoln was still, to outward appearances, a farming community. The view to the south from our new living room window centered on several large haystacks and the long low roof of a sprawling henhouse belonging to a prosperous chicken farm. Beyond, when the trees were bare in winter, one could see the square central chimney and shingled walls of one of Lincoln's oldest houses. North of us lay a dairy farm. We had arranged with the owner to rent him our pasture for a nominal sum if he would keep it in condition with an occasional application of cow manure, which — with concern for city folks' sensibilities — he politely referred to as "dressing." His low call of "Co' boss, co' boss," as he rounded up his herd for milking was one of the pleasantest sounds of a summer evening. No farmers ourselves, we housed from time to time hens, ducks, pigs, sheep, horses, and — for a brief period — Toggenburg goats: playful companions who unfortunately ate all the shrubbery. So situated, it was hard to think of ourselves as living in a suburb. But of course we were, and it was we and others like us, earning our living in the city, who made it so.

Though the subdivision regulations were new, Lincoln had adopted a zoning plan almost a decade earlier, one of the first towns in Massachusetts to do so. Passed by an overwhelming majority, it had set a minimum lot size of 10,000 square feet, or approximately a quarter of an acre: a modest beginning, but a recognition of the fact that haphazard uncontrolled growth would eventually destroy everything the town had stood for.

By its early adoption of zoning regulations and by its subsequent program of public land acquisition, Lincoln inevitably laid itself open to charges of social exclusiveness and snobbery, such as appeared, for example, in the Boston papers in earlier years when the large landowners fought the coming of the street railway. To certain people, even today, zoning is a dirty word. The very concept of protective ordinances to control the use of land, long since accepted in Europe, is considered somehow un-American. Yet by recognizing private land use as a public concern, the voters of Lincoln were reaffirming a principle that went back to the days of John Winthrop. In New England, as we have seen, land grants were from the beginning controlled by local authorities. Then it was a matter of maintaining a closely knit, responsible community in a wilderness where planned development was synonymous with survival. Now the danger was no longer one of starvation or Indian attack or weakening of the church fellowship. The threat was urban sprawl; and it was the speculator, not the savage, who had to be watched.

For towns immediately west of Boston, the opening of the new highway in 1934 brought the issue into sharp focus. Lincoln responded by framing a building code, and a subdivision law that increased the minimum lot size to one acre. No one who was in the town hall that March evening in 1936 when these regulations were adopted will ever doubt the effectiveness of the open town meeting in bringing about a consensus among citizens of disparate occupations and backgrounds. The town official who presented the motion took for granted the support of the commuters; he was speaking, he said, to the farmers — who were well represented on his committee — and he convinced them that the interest of the two groups were identical. When the vote came, it was unanimous.

A direction had been set. In dealing on an ad hoc basis with problems as they arose, the town had already chosen the course that it wanted to follow. The next step was to create some permanent machinery for keeping it on the beam. Conveniently, the Commonwealth of Massachusetts had just passed a Planning Act enabling towns to establish official Planning Boards. Lincoln promptly elected its first board — one of whose five members had, as his initial duty under the new law, called upon us that spring morning to set us politely upon the path of righteousness.

Population was growing, land values were rising, the farms and big estates were being broken up. Here as elsewhere, more families meant more schools and higher taxes.

The outbreak of World War II brought a temporary respite; for five years building virtually ceased. But the developers could afford to wait; it was a case of *reculer pour mieux sauter*. Beginning in the late forties, over ten million Americans moved to the suburbs within a single decade; "the greatest migration," declared a social historian, "in the shortest time in the nation's history." Quiet rural communities found themselves engulfed in an exodus from the city no less determined than the shad run upriver in spring. Building permits in Lincoln leaped from 7 in 1946 to 64 in 1947, and for a decade thereafter averaged about 50 a year. In 1955, to maintain some control over its growth rate, the town raised the minimum lot size to two acres. It was not a final solution, but it kept the bulldozers at bay while the people of Lincoln decided on what they wanted for the future — as a town, and as a part of the greater Boston community.

The pressing problem was the saving of open space: that is, land under cultivation or left in its natural state. This was not, as professional consultants pointed out, inconsistent with Lincoln's role in the larger community. "Different parts of a metropolitan region should be expected to serve different purposes, peculiar to the physical conditions, history and potentialities of the particular area." Open space should be acquired while that was still possible. Major wetlands should be preserved by conservation zoning. And in the interest of the whole community, there should be a system of "connected open spaces and public rights of way." Such a plan was, of course, the very opposite of exclusive. Conservation lands would be open to all, Lincoln residents and others alike. "No trespassing" signs would be replaced by trail markers and notices beginning, "You are welcome . . ." Like Henry Thoreau's beloved Old Marlborough Road, these woods and trails are places "where you may forget in what country you are travelling, where no farmer can complain that you are treading down his grass, no gentleman who has recently constructed a seat in the country that you are trespassing . . . where you can walk and think with the least obstruction, there being nothing to measure progress by, where you can pace when your breast is full, and cherish your moodiness . . . [where] you may hear a stake-driver, a whip-poor-will, a quail in a midsummer day . . ."

At best such a program would take years. As a start, a Conservation District was authorized to preserve wetlands against draining or building. A fund was started for land acquisition. A Conservation Commission was established, primarily to enable the town to use matching funds provided by the state and federal governments to encourage preservation of open land. In time the Commission would grow to become the guiding force in shaping the Lincoln landscape. The Lincoln Conservation Commission has now become a "farm manager," in the sense that it sees to the mowing, manuring, brush-cutting, etc., of the town's open lands. It also has the responsibility of reviewing subdivision plans which are submitted to the Planning Board.

Such were the first formal steps toward survival. Short of some immediate crisis, they might seem sufficient. But in land managment, crises are routine. Hence the necessity for a flexible, quick-acting organization, separate from the town government, that need not wait for the annual town meeting, that might at any time buy open land or receive it as a tax-deductible gift. In 1957, the Lincoln Land Conservation Trust was founded. "To promote the preservation of the rural character of the town, the development of walking and riding trails therein, and the establishment of sound conservation practices . . ."

The necessity for such practices is now generally accepted. Instead of further discussion of principles, let us look at visible results. This can best be done on foot.

It is early spring. The gently sloping pasture south of our house, now barely washed with green, is soft underfoot. Beyond an old stone wall lies a flat, damp field of rough meadow grass. A few weeks ago, it was half-covered with water, on which floated several black ducks and bright-plumed wood ducks; a few weeks hence, the ditch that runs

through it will be blue with wild flags and forget-me-nots. The higher ground to the west, bordering the town road, is already dry. There two girls in bright red jackets are cantering around a post-and-rail riding ring, doubtless preparing for the spring horse show of the 4-H Club; they share the field with meadowlarks, red-winged blackbirds, and a restless killdeer plover. Turning eastward, we enter a wood along a trail marked with small orange disks. Here young white pines are growing up where the hardwoods have been thinned — all of them apparently seeded by a solitary old pine that survived the devastating hurricane of 1938. Beside the trail the fiddleheads of young ferns are breaking through last year's leaves: at least seven species in one wet area a few yards square.

We are now on that little rise once known as Pigeon Hill, where, as mentioned earlier, flocks of passenger pigeons once rested in the great oaks. Through a gap in a stone wall, bordered by a stand of moccasin flowers, the path winds gently downward beside a maple swamp in which, judging from their persistent calls, a northern yellow-throat, a Canada warbler, and a flicker are staking out their territories. We come to a fork. One path (which would have all but disappeared were it not for the horseback riders) leads through a thicket of sheep laurel to a clearing that forty years ago was rich with highbush blueberries; since then, the maples and cedars and pines have shaded them out, and only a remnant of bird's-foot violets reminds us of earlier days. The other path borders the dark, heavily wooded swamp where, as my neighbor told me, the farm-ers of Lincoln once cut hay. Following the high ground, it circles back to emerge on an open hillside. Here, behind a sturdy dog-proof fence, a flock of sheep are grazing.

This short walk, which could be duplicated (with minor variations) in many parts of town, shows why so many de-vices are needed to accomplish the same end. The wet meadow and riding ring were once part of a farm. Develop-ment into house lots would have altered the entire land-scape and closed off the area forever to public use. With foresight, these fields had been marked in green on the town's land use map, for acquisition whenever they might become available. With 50 percent matching funds from the state, and half the remainder from the federal govern-ment, the town bought them for only twenty-five cents on the dollar. Shortly thereafter, the adjacent wet meadow and the maple swamp bordering Pigeon Hill were given to the town by their owners. But what of the woods, and the old blueberry field? Years before, they had been saved by a complex three-way operation, involving purchase by the Conservation Commission, gifts to the Land Trust, and zon-ing modifications by the Planning Board.

Finally, what of those sheep? When their hillside pasture suddenly came on the market over ten years ago, the five abutters were prepared to buy it to keep it open; but to divide it would have been too long and expensive a process. So each gave his share of the purchase price to the Land Trust, which then took title. The sheep, owned by one of the abutters, are still there, and anyone is welcome to walk on the land provided he controls his dog and closes the gates.

I make it sound too easy. Saving these woods and fields from haphazard development required delicate dovetailing by three conservation groups. It involved hours of private talk and public persuasion. Nor is the job of land-saving all sweetness and light. The bolder the program, the more vociferous the opposition. Witness that same town meeting at which a sour citizen heaped scorn on the woodchucks and the bluebirds. Up for public acquisition was a tract of over five hundred acres, a prime objective of the open space program from the start. It is a spectacularly beautiful area of rocky cliffs, clear streams and ponds; of meadows and cornfields and woodland trails running down to the Sudbury River. The Federal Bureau of Recreation had guaranteed matching funds to help the town preserve it for public use. One townsman, however, had a different idea. Here, he shouted into the microphone, is the perfect site for a country club. What a splendid golf course those cornfields would make! The whole thing could easily be paid for, he pointed out, by covering the rest of the land with custom-built, deluxe "homes," to sell at premium prices. "Keep talking!" members of the Conservation Commission silently prayed; "the longer you go on, the better." He talked for a long, long time, and the town now owns the land which, kept in its wild state, is used year round by visitors from the city.

Of course it is neither possible nor desirable to keep all remaining open land from being developed. The question is, what *kind* of development? To see that land which is going to be subdivided anyway is subdivided properly, a group of private citizens incorporated themselves as the Lincoln Rural Land Foundation. With a bank loan guaranteed by the members, the Foundation buys the land and employs its own landscape architect to make a subdivision plan, reserving a sizable tract of open space to be held for the public by the Land Trust. It then markets the lots, which, needless to say, are more attractive than they would be if a real estate speculator were trying to squeeze out the last penny of profit. From the beginning, this enterprise has worked without a hitch. The guarantors have never had to worry about their commitment. And since this is a nonprofit organization, any favorable balance constitutes a revolving fund to be applied again as need arises.

One major threat, however, is beyond local control. Everywhere in the suburbs, land prices are skyrocketing. Some older residents, who may have lived in town all their lives, have been squeezed out by rising taxes. Young couples can afford to move in only if they are well-to-do. Town employees, including schoolteachers, cannot afford to live where they work. Gazing into the crystal ball, one sees with a shudder a population of affluent middle-aged citizens, all of them (to quote Phyllis McGinley's *In Praise of Diversity*) "issuing one shrill, monotonous, level note." Was it for this that Simon Willard led his little band into the wilderness? Must the fine dreams of Chambers Russell, the crusty independence of Eleazer Brooks, end at last in dull monotony? Is it true, as some would have us believe, that the New England town is in itself an anachronism, and the sooner it is homogenized with the urban world, the better?

The burden of proving the contrary lies with the individual community. The drift is toward suburban sameness and tameness; to leeward, coming ever closer, lie the bland beaches of the wealthy bedroom town. If towns like Lincoln are to remain alive and afloat, they must constantly check their bearings — which means, in most cases, how they wish to use their land.*

The newest approach to land use in the suburbs is actually very old. What town planners call "cluster zoning" is the natural pattern of the English village, of the Italian hill town, of the original settlements in New England: closely grouped dwellings, surrounded by open land. Applied to new housing developments, it is a far more economical form of land use than dividing the entire acreage into individual house lots. Cluster zoning alone, however, does not answer the needs of those "honest and temperate men and women," as that early benefactor quaintly put it, "who work hard and are economical yet find it hard to make both ends meet." A major step in this direction, harking back to earlier times, was the decision to permit apartments in single-family dwellings. Such moves toward "holy heterodoxy" (in Miss McGinley's phrase) are enlightened but hardly revolutionary. The latest step was more radical. Several years ago, Lincoln faced up to the need for government-subsidized housing.

In the Town Report that year, the report of the Planning Board was entitled "A Letter to Our Grandchildren." "The thing we have always in our minds is that there will be alarmingly more of you than there are of us. Some of us were born here; most of us came here because it's beautiful and the air is fresh and we have green fields to walk in. We feel a terrible responsibility to see to it that as far as is humanly possible you will have a town like this to live in . . .

"And now we come to a matter of deepest concern . . . Land prices, even in our day, have risen beyond what most people can pay. We are thinking about you, and your teachers, and the police force and the firemen and the men who take care of our roads, and we are thinking about our-

* For further details on Lincoln's land use policy, see *Notes*, p. 262.

selves as we grow older and want a smaller, less costly home. We are determined to create some housing that anyone who really wants to live in Lincoln can afford."

But how? And where? Opinions differed, and emotions ran deep. What would be the impact of 125 families suddenly added to the town's population? Some bitterness, though seldom expressed, lay below the surface. We worked hard to get to Lincoln, a few people argued; why should we make it easy for these people? With exasperating slowness the problems were thrashed out, the plan approved, the land acquired. As I write, carpenters are framing the first of the housing units on a tract of woodland that once belonged to Chambers Russell. Across a small stream lies a broad cornfield stretching away to a maple swamp that is now reddening with the advance of spring. The field will be preserved as common land for the use of local residents; in John Winthrop's words, "for newcomers and for commons." During its long history, Lincoln has welcomed scores of "newcomers," some speaking foreign tongues, and made them its own. What was once natural and inevitable must now be planned. If it all works out as one hopes it will, the town may be different from what it is today, but it will be closer to what it once was.

As with the people, so with the land. Lincoln has been reluctant to accept the "sameness and tameness" that is too often the fate of the purely residential community. It has recognized the needs of the future. While the town-owned woods and wetlands are kept wild, the fertile fields are being put to the uses that God and the early settlers intended. As the new housing goes up, plows are preparing nearby acres, restored to agriculture as a community farm, for seeding. In another month they will be a checkerboard of browns and greens as more than a hundred family plots come under cultivation. By late summer, the vegetable stands and other local outlets will be doing a thriving busi-

ness. Hay cut on town fields, as part of the open space program, will be sold to local horse owners. Result, a self-
sustaining operation which proves that the soil in the
suburbs can be used for more than lawns and blacktop. If
farming here is no longer a way of life, neither is it a case
of Marie Antoinette playing shepherdess at Versailles.
Here, as in many other towns, the communal farm has
satisfied in practical terms the widespread yearning to re-
establish a human relationship to the land.

In every period of its history, Lincoln's leading citizens
have dealt as best they knew how with the challenges of
their time: to settle a wilderness, to build a town, to found
a nation, and always to make a living from the soil. As
farmers, they were smart enough to adjust to changing conditions, and they survived. Now that Lincoln has become a
suburb, the town fathers are dealing with problems un-
dreamed of in the past, but no less concerned with the land
itself. And the solutions must be even bolder and more
imaginative. By their very nature, town planning, zoning,
land-use regulations run head-on into the still common
concept that land is merely a marketable commodity, like
a used automobile or a share of stock. Owing to our frontier
tradition, we in America have been slower than most to
shake off what Henry Thoreau called the "groveling habit,
from which none of us is free," of regarding the soil as
property. As a contemporary scholar puts it: "the word
ownership is misleading. A person does not really own
land: he owns rights in land."

How he uses these rights will shape the character of the
community in which he lives. The speaker at the dedication of the Lincoln town hall knew this when he said that
a place was more than so many cubic feet of earth. The
original proprietors of the Bay Colony who so carefully divided up the common land as the colony grew, the farmers
who nurtured their fields and woodlots to pass on from

generation to generation understood the meaning of stewardship. They instinctively felt their land to be less a commodity than a trust. Though the farms are now few, the principle endures: a principle that once made, and can still make, the New England town a model for a happy marriage between man and the land.

NOTES AND SOURCES

Notes and Sources

CHAPTER I: A SENSE OF PLACE

Page 3. *Dedication of the Town House in Lincoln, Massachusetts, May 26, 1892* (Boston, 1893)

Page 3. *The Town of Lincoln, 1754–1904* (Lincoln, Massachusetts, 1905)

Page 5. "One family, for example." The Flint family.

Page 6. Lewis Mumford, *Sticks and Stones* (New York, 1924)

CHAPTER II: THE LIVING LANDSCAPE

A detailed description of the geology of the Lincoln area by J. W. Goldthwait is printed in the appendix to Charles Francis Adams' anniversary address, *A Milestone Planted.* (In *The Town of Lincoln, 1754–1904.*) Excellent interpretations of the New England scene will be found in *The Changing Face of New England* by Betty Flanders Thomson (New York, 1958) and in *A Guide to New England's Landscape* by Neil Jorgensen (Barre, Massachusetts, 1971).

Page 10. "high, level plain." The peneplain theory, which was generally accepted until recent times, is now being reconsidered.

Page 13. The "well-studied areas of Massachusetts" referred to is Petersham, site of the Harvard Forest. Professor Hugh M. Raup, its former director, is the author of a fascinating paper entitled, "The View from John Sanderson's Farm: A Perspective for the Use of the

Land" (*Forest History*, Vol. 10, No. 1, Forest History Society, Yale University).

Page 15. King's pines. The new royal charter for Massachusetts (including Plymouth, Maine, Nova Scotia and all land north to the St. Lawrence), issued in 1691, contained the following provision: "For the better providing and furnishing of Masts for Our Royal Navy, We do hereby reserve to Us, Our Heirs and Successors, all Trees of the Diameter of twenty four Inches, and upwards . . . growing up on any Soil or Tract of Land . . . not heretofore granted to any private Persons: And we do restrain and forbid all Persons whatsoever from felling, cutting or destroying such Trees without the Royal Licence of Us . . . upon Penalty of forfeiting *One Hundred Pounds* Sterling . . . for every such Tree so felled . . ."

Page 16. For these comments on the early settlers' reaction to the wilderness, I have relied particularly on Peter N. Carroll's *Puritanism and the Wilderness* (New York, 1969), and on Alan Heimert's essay, "Puritanism, the Wilderness and the Frontier" (New England *Quarterly*, XXXVI: 361–82).

Page 19. The sentence quoted at the end of the chapter (which is a major theme of this book) is from Carl Bridenbaugh's study entitled "The New England Town: A Way of Living" *American Antiquarian Society Proceedings*, LVI: 92).

CHAPTER III: THE FIRST "OWNERS"

Page 22. "The land-use philosophy of Indians . . ." Wilbur R. Jacobs, *Dispossessing the American Indian* (New York, 1972). Jacobs, like others before him, points out that "a part of our modern ecological awareness can certainly be traced to the historic land wisdom of the Indians . . . Henry David Thoreau, as much as any other writer of the nineteenth century, perceived that the white man misunderstood the woodland Indian . . . Thoreau recognized almost instinctively that primitive peoples the world over have much in common, especially in their closeness to nature and their remarkable ability to adapt their lives to the physical environment."

Page 22. "Recent apologists . . ." Alden T. Vaughan, *New England Frontier: Puritans and Indians* (Boston, 1965). Peter N. Carroll, *Puritanism and the Wilderness* (New York, 1969).

Page 23. William S. Ritchie, "The Indian and His Environment" (*New York Conservationist*, Dec.–Jan., 1955–56).

Page 23. Frank G. Speck, "Aboriginal Conservators" (*Birdlore*, 40: 258–61).

Page 24. "Though I cannot say . . ." Alexander Young, *Chronicles of the First Planters in the Colony of Massachusetts Bay* (Boston, 1846).

Page 25. Francis Higginson, *New England's Plantation* (1630).

Page 26. "Divine providence . . ." Thomas Morton quoted by Vaughan. Historians give various estimates of the date and the extent of the plague or plagues suffered by the Indians after the arrival of the first Europeans but before the founding of the Bay Colony. In *The Founding of New England*, edited by Stewart Mitchell, we read, "The plague of 1612 or thereabouts, is thought to have destroyed nine-tenths of the Indians of New England."

Page 26. "For the natives . . ." John Winthrop to Sir Nathaniel Rich, *Winthrop Papers*, III:167.

Page 26. Edward S. Morgan, *The Puritan Dilemma* (Boston, 1958).

Page 27. David Bushnell, "Indian Treatment in the Plymouth Colony," *N.E. Quarterly*, XXVI:193.

Indians in Lincoln. Richard J. Eaton, in the anniversary edition of *The Colonial* (June 24, 1954), notes that "the resident Indian population of the land within the boundaries of present-day Lincoln was exceedingly small and chiefly confined to the extreme westerly portion of the Town near the Sudbury River. Of the hundred and more sites that have been located in the Concord region, only seven are in Lincoln.

"Doubtless from their point of view, our rugged topography of hill, swamp, and rocky forest was only good for chestnuts, pigeons, turkeys and deer, all of which were within an hour's lope from their camps along the river."

On the other hand, in late 1646, eleven years after the founding of Concord, an agreement listing rules of conduct for the Indians vis-à-vis the English settlers concludes with the statement: "They [the Indians] desire they may be a towne, and either dwell on this side of Beaver Swamp, or at the East side of Mr. Flint's Pond." This is the year that the famous John Eliot, author of the Indian Bible, had been instructing them in the Christian religion, and their ostensible reason for wanting their own village so near the

English settlement was to be "ready to hear the word of God." Lemuel Shattuck, *History of the Town of Concord* (Boston, 1835).

CHAPTER IV: "AWAY UP IN THE WOODS"

This brief account of the founding of Concord is based principally on Lemuel Shattuck's *History of the Town of Concord* (Boston, 1835), Charles H. Walcott's *Concord in the Colonial Period* (Boston, 1885), Ruth M. Wheeler's *Concord: Climate for Freedom* (Concord, 1967), Townsend Scudder's *Concord: American Town* (Boston, 1947), and Albert E. Wood's essay, "The Plantation at Musketequid" [Wood insists on this spelling] (Concord Antiquarian Society, 1902). Early sources include Francis Higginson's *New England's Plantation* (1630), William Wood's *New England's Prospect* (1634), and Edward Johnson's *Wonder-Working Providence* (1651). The all-important matter of land use has been comprehensively dealt with by Melville Egleston in "The Land System of the New England Colonies" (*Johns Hopkins University Studies in Historical and Political Science*, Vol. XLV), and in Sumner Chilton Powell's *Puritan Village* (Middletown, Connecticut, 1963). For the quotation from Governor Sir Francis Bernard on p. 35 I am indebted to Paul Knight of the U.S. Department of the Interior.

The geology, soil, and natural features of the Concord region are well described in the introduction to *A Flora of Concord* by Richard J. Eaton (Cambridge, 1974) who also identified the grasses mentioned in the footnote on page 34.

Page 31. "First inland settlement." As Ruth Wheeler writes: "Concord was the first town carved out of the wilderness. Every other town in America had been close to the ocean or a tidal river, where goods could be transported by boat and natural features would mark the bounds with a minimum of exploration."

Page 36. Albert E. Wood, a civil engineer in Concord, traced the route of the early settlers by means of town records and his own knowledge of local topography. The route ran from Cambridge through Watertown and what is now Waverly, thence through the southern part of Lexington to Mill Street in Lincoln, and from there, by way of Virginia Road to Bedford Levels, Meriam's Corner, and the present Lexington Road (the old Bay Road) into Concord.

CHAPTER V: A TOWN IS BORN

The best printed source for the founding of Lincoln is Charles Francis Adams's address, *A Milestone Planted*, which was published (with amplifications) in the anniversary volume, *The Town of Lincoln, 1754–1904*. There is also a brief account by William F. Wheeler in Hamilton Hurd's *History of Middlesex County, Massachusetts*, 1890; and in Lemuel Shattuck's *History of the Town of Concord* (Boston, 1835), on which I have drawn for the account of the pastorate of the Reverend Daniel Bliss. The description of one of Bliss's revivalist sermons appeared in a letter to the Boston *Evening Post*, March 14, 1743.

For the early history of the church in Lincoln, see *The Lincoln Church Manual* by Henry Jackson Richardson (Boston, 1872), *One Hundred and Fiftieth Anniversary, First Church in Lincoln* by Edward E. Bradley, et al. (Cambridge, 1899), and the unpublished manuscript by the Reverend Charles M. Styron, "The First Parish in Lincoln," in the town library.

My principal source for this chapter, however, is the Lincoln *Precinct Records, 1746–1754*, supplemented by those of Concord and Lexington, and by the Journal of the House of Representatives.

Page 54. In his lack of enthusiasm for the war, the Reverend William Lawrence was scarcely typical of the New England clergy, many of whom became leaders of rebellion rather than voices of restraint. This was owing in part to their fear that the Church of England would attempt to impose Bishops on the Province. As the break with Britain approached, sermons had grown more and more political—perhaps an inevitable development when church and state were so closely allied. Concord's young minister, the Reverend William Emerson (Ralph Waldo Emerson's grandfather), was militant enough to satisfy the most warlike of his flock. When war broke out, he served the army as chaplain, and died at the age of thirty-three on his way home from Ticonderoga.

Lincoln's first pastor was fifteen years older than Emerson and of a very different stamp. As early as the autumn of 1774, during those tense months following the closing of the Port of Boston, the Lincoln congregation became divided against itself on the highly charged issue of their pastor's patriotism. To the indignation of Lawrence and his supporters, the local Committee of Safety went so far as to intercept his mail, and on one occasion he was almost prevented from conducting the Sabbath service. Though his enemies never succeeded in proving him a Tory, the suspicion hung over him almost to the time of his death in 1780. In Lawrence's own handwriting, though not a part of the official church record, is an account of several parish meetings "upon ye subject of some uneasiness subsisting in the minds of some of ye brethren of their Pastor," namely, that he "had not been friendly to his Country in respect to ye contest between Greate Brittain and America." The meetings dragged on for months. Finally it was decided to drop the affair since the evidence "on examination appeared trifling and insufficient for ye purpose." Possibly it was nothing more than the fact that Lawrence's oldest daughted had just married Dr. Joseph Adams, an openly professed Tory who left the country to make his home in England.

More than a century later, the minister of the Lincoln church, Reverend Edward E. Bradley, in recounting its early history, felt obliged to explain away on the grounds of ill health Dr. Lawrence's "failure to take an active part in the public movements of those stirring times," in contrast to Concord's William Emerson and Lexington's Jonas Clark.

Page 56. Governor Shirley had other reasons for not wanting to exacerbate his relations with the Legislature. Anticipating renewed hostilities with the French, he was anxious to get support for his military ventures. The following year he became commander of all the British forces on the continent.

Page 57. In his address at the dedication of the new town hall, William Everitt suggested an additional reason for the name "Lincoln."

"The contemporary records state that the name of Lincoln was given to this town at the suggestion of its honored citizen, Chambers Russell, whose ancestors had come more than a century before from Lincolnshire in England. Without disputing this statement, I must believe that the name was accepted by Governor Shirley because it fell in with the practice of naming our towns after the noblemen high in the councils of Great Britain at the time. Very shortly before the incorporation of your town had died the prime minister of England, Henry Pelham, and it was understood that his power would pass to his brother, Thomas Pelham, Duke of Newcastle. The town of Pelham received its name in 1742, and New Castle in Maine in 1753. Now the heir of the Pelhams was their nephew, Henry Pelham, Earl of Lincoln, at that time high in employment with George II; and I cannot doubt that Mr. Russell's ancestral recollections of considerably over a century old were much refreshed by the courtier-like propriety of selecting the name of Lincoln."

CHAPTER VI: A WAY OF LIFE

Page 60. Vernon L. Parrington, *Main Currents in American Thought* (New York, 1927).

Page 60. Thomas Jefferson, *Notes on the State of Virginia*, 1784–1785.

Page 60. J. Hector St. John Crèvecoeur, *Letters from an American Farmer* (1782).

Page 61. "Surviving inventories . . ." Town of Lincoln, *Assessor's Records.*

Page 61. Indian corn. Percy W. Bidwell and John I. Falconer, *History of Agriculture in the Northern United States* (New York, 1925, 1941).

Page 62. Ann Leighton, *Early American Gardens* (Boston, 1970).

Page 62. Colonial garden. S. G. Goodrich, *Recollections,* in *Land that Our Fathers Plowed,* David B. Greenberg, ed. (Norman, Oklahoma, 1969).

Page 62. ". . . varieties of soil . . ." John Warner Barber, *Historical Collections* (Worcester, 1839).

Page 63. Ricardo Torres Keyes, *Farming and Land Uses* (National Park Service).

Page 64. American Husbandry, Anonymous (London, 1775).

Page 64. Alice M. Earle, *Customs and Fashions in Old New England* (New York, 1893).

Page 64. "James Barrett of Concord . . ." Albert E. Wood, *How Our Great-grandfathers Lived* (Concord Antiquarian Society).

Page 66. "A typical house . . ." S. G. Goodrich, *Recollections.*

Page 67. John Brinckerhoff Jackson, *Landscapes* (University of Massachusetts Press, 1970).

Page 68. Bounty on crows. Lincoln *Town Records,* March 7, 1791.

Page 69. Thoreau, *Journal,* March 4, 1859; March 23, 1856; 1850.

Page 70. Thomas Jefferson Wertenbaker, *The First Americans* (New York, 1927).

Page 70. W. B. Weedon, *Economic and Social History of New England 1620–1789* (Boston, 1890).

Page 71, note. Thoreau, *Journal*, November 20, 1853; October 27, 1853.

Page 72. Thoreau, *Journal*, October 20, 1853.

Page 73. Noah Porter, *The New England Meeting House* (New Haven, 1933).

Page 73. Page Smith, *As a City Upon a Hill: the Town in American History* (New York, 1966).

Page 74. "Good harde wine." *Winthrop Papers*, III:166. In 1648 Emmanuel Downing wrote to his "Cosin [sic] John Winthrop Jr.: 'I have now sold my horse to James Oliver for 10 li [pounds] to purchase the still. I pray remember me about the German receipt for making strong water with Rye meall without maulting the Corne.' " (V: 230).

Page 76. John Olin Eidson, *Charles Stearns Wheeler: Friend of Emerson* (Athens, Georgia, 1951).

Page 76. Edward G. Porter, in *One Hundred and Fiftieth Anniversary, First Church in Lincoln*.

CHAPTER VII: EMBATTLED FARMERS

Page 85. Like Eleazer Brooks, Concord's pastor, Reverend William Emerson, considered himself a loyal British subject, despite his devotion to the cause of the colonies. A month before the battle at the bridge he delivered a "Sermon upon the present military manoevres in Concord" in which he said, "Then shall it be known that what we do this Day, was from cordial Affection and True Loyalty to our rightful Sovereign King George the Third." (William Emerson, *Diaries and Letters*, arranged by Amelia Forbes, privately printed).

Page 90. "Spies kept the British well informed . . ." The quotation is from *A Journal kept by Mr. John Howe, while he was employed as a British spy, during the Revolutionary War* (Concord, New Hampshire, 1827). Continuing the account of this visit, Howe refers to one of the few Tory families in Lincoln. "I asked the old man if there were any tories nigh there; he said there was one tory house in sight, and he wished it was in flames; I asked him what the man's name was; he said it was Gove. I very well knew where I was now, being the very house I wanted to find, it was situated in Lincoln, about four miles from Concord. Mr. Gove being one of His Majesty's friends. Here the old gentleman told the old lady to put some balls in the bullet pouch; she asked him how many; he said thirty or forty, perhaps I shall have an opportunity to give some to them that have not got any. The old woman pulled out an old drawer, and went to picking out — the old man says, old woman put in a handful of buck shot, as I understand the English like an assortment of plumbs. Here I took leave of the old gentleman and lady, and set off, the sun being about on hour high. I travelled on the Lexington road about one mile, then I turned out west for Mr. Gove's house, arrived there about half an hour after sunset."

Page 91. Excellent amounts of the events of April 18–19 will be found in such books as Esther Forbes's *Paul Revere and the World He Lived In*; Frank W. Coburn's *The Battle of April 19, 1775*; Allen French's *The Day of Concord and Lexington*; Harold Murdock's *The Nineteenth of April, 1775*; Arthur B. Tourtellot's *William Diamond's Drum*, and in *The Lexington-Concord Battle Road*, as compiled by the late Edwin W. Small. The events that occurred within the boundaries of Lincoln have been lovingly recorded, from personal reminiscences as well as from documents, in F. W. C. Hersey's booklet, *Heroes of the Battle Road*.

Page 92. ". . . aware that they were making history." On April 30, 1775, Reverend William Emerson noted in his journal: "This Month remarkable for the greatest Events taking Place in the Present Age."

Page 92. ". . . spring has come a month early." In her history of Bedford, Massachusetts, *Wilderness Town*, Louise K. Brown writes: "Spring had come early in that year [1775], so early that the advanced season was to make history itself. Farmers had been plowing and seeding the fields weeks ahead of the usual time. The winter rye was up so high that a Woburn Minuteman recorded 'it waved like grass as we crossed the fields to Lexington.' " However, contrary to tradition, the day itself was cool. Professor John Winthrop of Harvard, who kept meterological records for many years, recorded April 19 as "fair with clouds," the thermometer rising only to 50°. Other local observers noted that the weather was clear, with a fresh wind from the west. See "Weather 200 Years Ago" by David Ludlum, *Country Journal*, April, 1975.

Page 102. There are two conflicting accounts of Mary Hartwell's actions on April 19. In his *Heroes of the Battle Road*, Hersey has

her taking her children for safety to her father's house in Lincoln
Center before the British retreat from Concord, and returning to
the farm early the following morning. His source is evidently her
grandson, Jonas Hartwell. On the other hand, Samuel Hartwell,
another grandson, gave an interview to the Boston *Globe* on April
15, 1894, in which he quoted his grandmother's own words, telling
how she saw from the Hartwell homestead the British returning
disorganized and "wild with rage," and how they fired shots into
the house as they went by, fortunately missing her and the children.
Both accounts agree, however, about her following the ox-cart with
the dead British soldiers the following morning, and watching them
being interred in a common grave.

In 1850 Henry Thoreau wrote in his journal: "I visited a retired,
now almost unused, graveyard in Lincoln to-day, where five British
soldiers lie buried who fell on the 19th of April, '75. Edmund
Wheeler . . . went over the next day and carted them to this
ground. A few years ago one Felch, a phrenologist, by leave of
the Selectmen dug up and took away two skulls. The skulls were
very large, probably those of grenadiers."

CHAPTER VIII: THE PRICE OF WAR

The principal source for this chapter is the Lincoln *Town Records*.
For contemporaneous events in Concord, I have relied chiefly on
Townsend Scudder's *Concord: American Town*.

CHAPTER IX: ELEAZER BROOKS: THE PEACEMAKER

This chapter is based almost entirely on the Eleazer Brooks Papers
(now in the Lincoln Town Library), supplemented by Shattuck
and by the Lincoln church histories. Special thanks are due to
Harriet Rogers, who lives in the Eleazer Brooks house and who
Xeroxed and indexed the papers, and to Margaret Flint, who provided me with the Brooks family genealogy, along with other
material on early Lincoln.

CHAPTER X: BACK TO BEGINNINGS

A principal source for the background material in this chapter is
Town Government in Massachusetts (1620–1930) by John F. Sly

(Cambridge, 1930). Other sources include *Three Episodes of Massachusetts History* by Charles Francis Adams (Boston, 1892), a symposium on "New England Town Origins," edited by H. B. Adams, et al. (*Massachusetts Historical Society Proceedings*, VII: 174), "Freemanship in Puritan Massachusetts," by B. Katherine Brown (*American Historical Review*, LIX: 865), and articles by Edward Channing and Jared Sparks in *Johns Hopkins University Studies in Historical and Political Science* (II: 5, and XVI: 579). Two individual town histories are of particular interest: Kenneth A. Lockridge's *A New England Town, the First Hundred Years: Dedham, Mass., 1636–1736* (New York, 1970), and Philip J. Greven's *Four Generations: Andover* (Ithaca, New York, 1970).

The quotations on pages 143 and 147, dealing with the duties of town officials, are from a surprisingly readable volume entitled *Town Officer, or Laws of Massachusetts* by Isaac Goodwin (Worcester, 1829).

The Lincoln material is taken directly from the town records.

CHAPTER XI: TOWN MEETING TONIGHT

This chapter is based almost entirely on the Lincoln and Concord town records, supplemented by John F. Sly's *Town Government in Massachusetts (1620–1930)*, Cambridge, 1930, and Page Smith's *As a City Upon a Hill* (New York, 1966), which includes an interesting discussion of the origins of our democratic system.

Page 155. The other four Selectmen — in addition to Ephraim Flint — were Ephraim Hartwell, Ebenezer Cutler, Samuel Farrar, and John Hoar.

CHAPTER XII: MIDPASSAGE

Sources include the Lincoln town meeting records, tax lists, vital statistics, and the annual reports of the town committees.

Page 167. "Their own parish." The bitter dispute between the "liberals" and the orthodox members of the (still Calvinistic) Congregational Church, which led to the growth of Unitarianism, had its beginnings in Boston and surrounding towns early in the century. In 1819 Dr. William Ellery Channing summarized the objections to the orthodox theology: "By exhibiting a severe and partial Deity, it tends strongly to pervert the moral faculty, to form a gloomy, forbidding, and servile religion, and to lead men to substitute censoriousness, bitterness, and persecution for a tender and impartial charity." Quoted by M. A. DeWolfe Howe in *Boston, the Place and the People* (New York, 1903.) Yet less than twenty years later Unitarianism had established an orthodoxy of its own from which individualists like Emerson felt obliged to separate themselves.

Page 167. "When separation came . . ." In 1833 the Massachusetts law formally separated the functions of church and town.

Page 167. The Episcopal Church in Lincoln was founded in 1874, the Roman Catholic Church in 1904.

Page 170. Codman Farm. The mansion house now belongs to the Society for the Preservation of New England Antiquities. The barns and most of the farmland have been acquired by the town for public purposes. (See note, p. 263.) In a unique and fascinating study based on thousands of family papers, R. Curtis Chapin has traced the history of the property and the "major renovation and expansion of a small Georgian-style mansion . . . into a grand Federal-styled country seat," which is considered by experts to be "one of the most important houses in New England."

Page 176. The cemetery in the original Flint field, now the town's principal cemetery, dates from Lincoln's founding in 1754; the one behind the town hall from 1767 (or earlier); the three-cornered cemetery at Lexington, Old Lexington, and Trapelo Roads, from 1820.

Page 178. The Scipio Bristor buried in the Lincoln cemetery was a servant in the Hoar family, of Hoar's Tavern in Lincoln on the Concord Turnpike. On April 19, 1775, he and young Leonard Hoar, left at home to guard the women and children, gave food and drink to the American militia as they passed through in pursuit of the British. As Lincoln historian Betty Little has pointed out, Thoreau confused this Bristor (who apparently never married) with Bristor of Bristor's Hill in Concord, married to Fenda, and listed as "Bristor Freeman" in the 1790 Concord census.

Page 183. The Harvard professor referred to is John Farrar, who was born in Lincoln in 1779 and died in 1853. He held a professorship in mathematics and natural philosophy, and was a scholar of international reputation. His widow, Mrs. Eliza Farrar, author of *A Manual for Young Ladies* and *Recollections of Seventy Years*, left his books to Lincoln "for the purpose of forming part of a public library." See *Proceedings at the Dedication of the Lincoln Library* (Cambridge, 1884).

Page 183. The donor of the library building was George Grosvenor Tarbell, a native of Lincoln who "after a successful business career, returned to the home of his childhood."

CHAPTER XIII: MAN AND NATURE IN CONCORD

The principal sources for this chapter are the journals of Emerson, Thoreau, and Alcott; Hawthorne's *American Notebooks;* and Perry Miller's selection from the writings of Margaret Fuller, together with numerous biographies, of which Walter Harding's comprehensive *The Days of Henry Thoreau* (New York, 1965) is particularly valuable as a reference. Thoreau's opinions on various subjects are conveniently presented by Edwin Way Teale in *The Thoughts of Thoreau* (New York, 1962). Van Wyck Brooks's *The Flowering of New England* (New York, 1936) contains several lively chapters on the Concord literary renaissance.

Page 199. "Moralizing from nature came easily to Emerson; Thoreau increasingly saw it as a weakness." Samuel Taylor Coleridge had already expressed much the same view as Thoreau, in a letter to a friend in 1802: ". . . never to see or describe any interesting appearance in nature, without connecting it by dim analogies with the moral world, proves faintness of Impression. Nature has her proper interest; & he will know what it is, who believes & feels, that every Thing has a Life of it's own, & that we are all *one Life.* A Poet's *Heart & Intellect* should be *combined, intimately combined & unified,* with the great appearances in Nature—& not merely held in solution & loose mixture with them, in the shape of formal Similes."

Page 214. Estabrook Woods. William K. Newbury of Harvard's Museum of Comparative Zoology summarizes as follows a history of man's use of the Estabrook Woods, compiled by Desmond Fitzgerald from documents dating back to the 1640s: "The earliest inhabitants of the town stuck close to the rivers but, as the population expanded, people soon moved into the wooded upland areas. By 1700 much of the Estabrook Woods had been cleared for use as 'common' pasture land. This cooperative use, however, soon gave way to the system based on private ownership of small parcels, a system symbolized by the network of stonewalls which still exists today.

Though the soil was poor, the farmers who owned these plots worked the land for more than a century, turning much of the remaining woodland into gardens and orchards.

"The decline of agriculture at the beginning of the nineteenth century led to the rise in importance of wood products and recreational use of the Woods. For example, Henry David Thoreau's family established its pencil factory there to take advantage of the cedars that had colonized the abandoned fields. According to Thoreau's remarks in his journal, by the 1850's the Woods had also become a favorite place for picnickers and hikers.

"As the forest matured in the latter half of the century, more and more trees were cut for fuelwood to heat homes in Concord, Boston and surrounding communities. After the development of central heating early in the 1900's, cutting for firewood decreased rapidly. Recreational use of the Woods, however, has continued and is in fact now rapidly growing due to the increasing popularity of cross country skiing."

CHAPTER XIV: TWO WORLDS MEET

Page 220. The comments of the change in the appearance of Lincoln are in the address of Edward I. Smith at the dedication of the new town hall.

Page 222. Sumner Smith recalls the hearing held in the town hall to give the citizens a chance to be heard on the plans for the street railway: "The selectmen, consisting of my father [Charles Sumner Smith], Edward Flint and John F. Farrar as chairman sat on the stage to hold the hearing. For a small town it contained prominent talent in the legal field. Moorfield Storey, Charles Francis Adams, Henry Warner were some of the main arguers for the town. The purpose seemed to be to tie up the railroad fellows so they wouldn't know which way they were going. I remember John Farrar kept going to sleep that night. My father kept nudging him to keep him awake. That didn't help him any in the next campaign for selectman."

Page 223. When the new town hall was erected, the original building, constructed in 1848, was purchased by George Chapin for use as a store, and moved to the west side of Bedford Road, uphill from the white church. On Chapin's death, Charles S. Smith bought it and moved it to its present site, where it provided quarters for both a grocery store and the Lincoln Center post office. The building has been permanently preserved through purchase, in 1962, by the Old Town Hall Corporation. It is currently occupied by the Center post office, the old Town Hall Exchange, and professional offices.

Page 223. In 1904 Henry Lee Higginson had bought for his son, A. Henry Higginson, the old Jacob Baker farm, near the corner of Baker Bridge and Walden roads. The latter published his hunting reminiscences under the title *Try Back* (New York, 1931). In addition to his splendid stables, rebuilt by his father after a disastrous fire in 1914, he had a race track on his estate.

Page 224. "New town hall . . ." The bequest of George Flint Bemis financed the construction of the new town hall and endowed the lecture series, free to residents of Lincoln, known as the Bemis Free Lectures. They are administered by a board of trustees elected by the town.

Page 224. Drumlin Farm, headquarters of the Massachusetts Audubon Society since 1959, and the Hathaway School of Conservation Education were established through a bequest from Mrs. Conrad Hathaway.

Page 225. Pierce House and Pierce Park — which contributes so much to the feeling of openness of the town center — were left to the town by John H. Pierce. The original purpose was to establish a hospital, which proved to be impractical.

Page 226. For the full story of de Cordova and the museum, see the booklet entitled *The Life and Mind of Julian de Cordova,* by Herbert Levine. There is also a good deal on the subject in Boston newspaper files.

Julian de Cordova got his start in business as an associate of his father-in-law, Thomas Dana, a leading wholesale grocer in Boston. The complete name of the museum is the De Cordova and Dana Museum and Park.

Page 229. See *The Turnpikes of New England* by Frederick J. Wood (Boston, 1919).

Page 229. The "influential townsman and state representative" referred to here was George Grosvenor Tarbell, son of the donor of the Lincoln Library. It was also George Tarbell who presented so effectively the motion for one-acre zoning at the 1936 town meeting (see p. 234).

CHAPTER XV: ROOM FOR LIVING

Page 235. The quotations are from *Planning for Lincoln* by Charles W. Eliot and Planning and Research Associates (December, 1958), popularly known as the "Braun-Eliot Report." A still more comprehensive development plan, *Land Use in Lincoln*, prepared by Adams, Howard and Oppermann (the "By '70 Report"), was issued in 1965.

Page 236. The first Conservation District, approved by the town in 1960, was established on a purely voluntary basis: i.e., individual landowners accepted a permanent restriction (which runs with the land) against draining, filling, or building up the wetland areas of their property. This initial district involved the central drainage area surrounding Beaver Pond. Comprehensive and compulsory wetland zoning, which includes some 1300 acres throughout the town, was adopted in 1974.

Page 236. "A fund was started for land acquisition." It is important to note that open land has been purchased by the town at its full market value. The full sum must be voted at town meeting, by a two-thirds majority. Later the town receives reimbursement from the state and/or the federal government, running as high as 75 percent of the purchase price when both sources are available.

Page 236. Robert A. Lemire, current chairman of the Lincoln Conservation Commission, has summarized the town's land use policy as follows: "Lincoln comprises some 5000 residents on 9500 acres of land. Of these, 900 acres have been bought since 1960 by the Conservation Commission for some $2¼ million. Of this, roughly $1 million has been reimbursed by the Federal Government and some $600 thousand by the State. The $600 thousand balance has been bonded over an average of 10 years and is impacting our tax rate by roughly $1 out of $65. In other words, it costs an average family some $25 to $30 per year for 10 years. Our town is assessed for some $50 million so basically we've made a net commitment of roughly 1% to assure a balanced setting to our real estate.

"We bought the land because it was on the market and would otherwise have been developed. It could be argued that given our zoning at time of purchase we preempted some 250 potential house lots. It can be demonstrated, however, that the tax revenue to be derived from new housing does not, on the average, cover the cost of the additional town services that will be required. In a stable society, the average family pays to the community roughly the equivalent of what it gets in the form of services. Consider, for example, a young man getting married at age 21, moving into a former neighbor's house. For some seven years he pays taxes and costs little. As his children enter and leave school, his family costs more than it pays. Later he makes it up. Something else happens when a bedroom community develops. New houses are built. More money is spent on schools and roads, on police and fire protection and so on. By the time it's over, you get what happened to Lincoln between 1950 and 1970 — the population doubles and tax levy goes up by a factor of 15. As the dynamics of this process develop, agricultural land is forced into development and the rural element is driven out.

"Now the people don't do this to fellow citizens on purpose. It is a result of antiquated zoning and subdivision restrictions. Having become aware of this, we have reworked our zoning to accommodate growth in our community without over-burdening existing residents, to make certain that the remaining dwelling units implied in our zoning are essentially consistent with the number we see as the town's carrying capacity. In short, we are convinced that the limited future growth we foresee in Lincoln will allow us to retain our remaining rural character while permitting a diverse social and economic mix, control per capita taxes, maintain good schools while sharing them with urban children, and sustain the productivity of our agricultural lands. Through wetland zoning, we can meet our own needs for water as well as those of neighboring urban areas. (Being at the top of a watershed, Lincoln and its environs provide about two-thirds of Cambridge's water.) Finally, we feel this low-density strategy has ethical merit because it retains the natural attributes of a beautiful and historically important area in a way that makes it available to the general public.

"All of this is not to say that we no longer have any problems. It does mean that we do have a way of dealing with the wave of change that is moving through our area with assurance that we will still have a town when the wave passes.

Page 241. A Letter to Our Grandchildren was written by Susan M. Brooks, chairman of the Planning Board.

Page 242. Codman Community Farms, Inc., was established in 1973 for the purpose of continuing the agricultural tradition which

shaped Lincoln for two centuries. The participation of residents
of all ages throughout the town has resulted in a rapidly expanding
operation. In addition to the family garden plots, projects include
a market garden, haying, raising sheep and beef cattle, beekeeping,
maple-sugaring, and other activities. Once part of "The Grange,"
the Codman family's country seat, Codman Farm is heir to almost
250 years of documented agricultural history.

Page 243. Anthony Lewis, writing from England for the *New
York Times* (June 10, 1972), describes the success of national zoning legislation in saving the villages in parts of East Anglia (from
which came so many of the early settlers in New England): "The
people accept that there are values overriding the rights of private
property. They do without big new hotels and speculative housing
developments marching across the moors; they prefer the moors.
When there is that feeling, the legislation works; places remain
themselves.

"So the villages of East Suffolk, remote as they may feel from
the world of power, have something to say to America and other
places facing the pressures of population and affluence. It is possible
to resist those pressures. A community can remain true to itself if
pride in its integrity is stronger than the desire to exploit private
property. And it is not just local matter; there is a national interest
in treating genuine communities as a resource for the whole nation,
in putting them ahead of passing profit."

Page 243. A penetrating study entitled *Rights of Ownership or
Rights of Use?* by Professor Lynton K. Caldwell appeared in Massachusetts Audubon Society's *Man and Nature,* 1975, reprinted from
the *William and Mary Law Review.*

INDEX

Index